Dr. Del's Tier 2

Notes and Exercises

Not Intended for Self-Study

Tutorial Videos for each Lesson are available to expedite the learning.

Craig Hane, Ph.D.
Triad Math, Inc.

Dr. Del's Tier 2 Notes and Exercises

Not Intended for Self-Study

By: Craig Hane, Ph.D.

© 2023 Triad Math, Inc. All Rights Reserved

No part of this publication may be reproduced or transmitted in any form or by any means, including photocopying and recording, or by any information storage and retrieval system, without permission in writing form the author or publisher (except by a reviewer, who may quote brief passages and/or show brief video clips in a review)

Disclaimer: Publisher and the Author make no representations or warranties with respect to the accuracy or completeness of the contents of this work and specifically disclaim all warranties, including without limitation warranties of fitness for a particular purpose. No warranty may be created or extended by sales or promotional materials. The advice and strategies contained herein may not be suitable for every situation. This work is sold with the understanding that the Publisher is not engaged in the rendering of any professional services. Neither the Publisher nor the Author shall be liable for damages arising herefrom. The fact that an organization or website is referred to in this work as a citation and/or a potential source of further information does not mean that the Author or Publisher endorses the information the organization or website may provide or recommendations it may make. Further, readers should be aware that internet websites listed in this work may have changed or disappeared between then this work was written and when it is read.

2023 Edition

Published by:
Triad Math, Inc.
3822 S. Westmont Ave., Bloomington, IN 47403, US
Phone: 01-812-355-3030 ext. 402
Email: info@TriadMathInc.com
www.TriadMathInc.com

Foreword

These are the Notes and Exercises for Dr. Del's Tier 2 Online Math Program for post-elementary students.

The student should be studying these Lessons in a consecutive sequence with the Tutorial Videos and Quizzes.

This book is designed to be used by a student who has access to a good math teacher/tutor or is enrolled in Del's Tier 2 Online Math Program.

You may purchase access to the Dr. Del's Tier 2 Online Math Program Tutorial Videos, if you have not already done so, by emailing info@TriadMathInc.com or by visiting HomeSchoolerToday.com.

Triad Math, Inc. © 2023

Revised 2023-01-10

Craig Hane, Ph.D., Founder

Tier 2 Notes

INTRODUCTION TO ALGEBRA

Algebra is a "technology" for finding unknown numbers, X, Y, Z, etc., from known numbers **A, B, C**, etc. In our Foundation course, we will only deal with one unknown number, usually denoted X, but we could denote it with any symbol.

The Algebra technique is to create an Equation involving the unknown number X and the known numbers **A, B, C**, etc., based on their known relationships and then "solving" the equation for the unknown, and checking the answer.

Step 1 is to "**create**" the equation between X and the knowns.

Step 2 is to "**solve**" this equation by finding out what value of X makes the equation true when substituted for X.

Step 3 is to "**verify**" or "**check**" the solution by making the substitution.

Simple Example: [Word Problem] Three years from now Mary will be twice as old as Joe who is 7 years old today. How old is Mary now?

Step 1. Let X be Mary's age today. This is the unknown we want to find. In three years Mary will be $X + 3$ years old. In three years Joe will be $7 + 3 = 10$ years old. So, we are given that in three years $X + 3 = 2 \times 10 = 20$

Step 2. Solve the equation. By trial and error, it appears **17** might be the answer.

Step 3. Check. Substitute 17 for X. $17 + 3 = 20$. So, **17** is the answer.

Now, in general, it is not too hard to do Step 1. Define what **X** stands for and then relate the given facts to X and create an equation.

Step 2 can be very easy; or, very difficult, to solve. In the Foundation course, we will deal with equations that arise in many common situations, and these are usually easy to solve.

Step 3 is quite easy with a calculator.

1.1 Lessons Abbreviation Key Table

A = Algebra Lesson
G = Geometry Lesson
T = Trigonometry Lesson

The number following the letter is the Lesson Number.
E = Exercises with Answers: Answers are in brackets [ ].
EA = Exercise Answers: (only used when answers are not on the same page as the exercises.)
ES = Exercise Supplemental: Complete if you feel you need additional problems to work.

1.2 Exercises Introduction

Why do the Exercises?

Mathematics is like a "game." The more you practice and play the game the better you will understand and play it.

The Foundation's Exercises, which accompany each lesson, are designed to reinforce the ideas presented to you in that lesson's video.
It is unlikely you will learn math very well by simply reading about it or listening to Dr. Del, or anyone else, or watching someone else doing it.

You WILL learn math by "doing math."

It is like learning to play a musical instrument, or write a book, or play a sport, or play chess, or cooking.

You will learn by practice.

Repetition is the key to mastery.

You will make mistakes. You will sometimes struggle to master a concept or technique. You may feel frustration sometimes "WE ALL DO."

But, as you learn and do math, you will begin to find pleasure and enjoyment in it as you would in any worthwhile endeavor. Treat it like a sport or game.

These Exercises are the KEY to your SUCCESS!

ENJOY

A1 LESSON: FOUR WAYS TO SOLVE AN ALGEBRA EQUATION

Suppose you have an equation with one unknown, X. How can you solve it?

There are essentially four ways.

1. **Guess the answer**. Check to see if you are right. This is a good way with really simple equations. It can be the best way with very complicated equations **IF** you have a computer to help. This is then called **Numerical Analysis**.

2. **Apply a Formula**. This is fine **IF** you know an appropriate formula. This is useful if you are solving the same type of equation frequently and have the formula available. However, it can be quite difficult to find or remember the correct formula. Formulas are often given in Handbooks for special situations.

3. **Apply a Process**. This is the best way for certain equations, and it is how we will solve most of our equations in this Foundation course, and in the real world.

4. **Apply a Power Tool**. This is the best way for complex equations. One great tool for this is Mathematica. This is how engineers solve most of their equations. But, you must learn to use this tool first. We will cover it extensively in the upper Tiers in our advanced training. If also applies to other types of equations.

In our Foundation course, we will learn to **Apply a Process**. This usually is easier than trying to find the correct formula. It is faster and more accurate for certain types of equations we will be dealing with.

Four Ways to Solve an Algebra Equation

Suppose you have an equation with one unknown, X. How can you solve it?

What are the Four Ways to solve an equation?

1.

2.

3.

4.

Which way will be utilize and learn in the Foundations Course? Why?

Four Ways to Solve an Algebra Equation

Suppose you have an equation with one unknown, X. How can you solve it?

What are the Four Ways to solve an equation?

1. **Guess the answer**. Check to see if you are right. This is a good way with really simple equations. It can be the best way with very complicated equations IF you have a computer to help. This is then called Numerical Analysis.

2. **Apply a Formula**. This is fine **IF** you know an appropriate formula. This is useful if you are solving the same type of equation frequently and have the formula available. However, it can be quite difficult to find or remember the correct formula. Formulas are often given in Handbooks for special situations.

3. **Apply a Process**. This is the best way for certain equations, and it is how we will solve most of our equations in this Foundation course, and in the real world.

4. **Apply a Power Tool**. This is the best way for complex equations. One great tool for this is Mathematica. This is how engineers solve most of their equations. But, you must learn to use this tool first. We will cover it extensively in the upper Tiers in our advanced training. If also applies to other types of equations.

Which way will be utilize and learn in the Foundations Course? Why?

In our Foundation course, we will learn to **Apply a Process**. This usually is easier than trying to find the correct formula. It is faster and more accurate for certain types of equations we will be dealing with.

Four Ways to Solve an Algebra Equation

1. In the PMF, what do we want to know about an Algebra Equation?

2. Why do we normally use Applying a Process instead of Applying a Formula to solve algebra equations?

Four Ways to Solve an Algebra Equation   Answers: [ ]

2. In the PMF, what do we want to know about an Algebra Equation?

[We want to see if we can find the value of the unknown in the equation, most generally denoted by X!]

3. Why do we normally use Applying a Process instead of Applying a Formula to solve algebra equations?

[Applying a Formula only works for special types of problems and specific formulas, and requires a good deal of memorization. Applying a Process allows us to work with many types of equations with needing to memorize specific formulas!]

A2 LESSON: THE RULE OF ALGEBRA

Suppose we have an equation to solve. It will have a Left Side (**LS**) and a Right Side (**RS**) either of which might contain the unknown, **X**, and other known numbers. (Any letter could be the unknown.)

Equation: **LS = RS**   Can switch sides   **RS = LS**

THE RULE of Equation Solving is: You may do the same thing to both sides of the equation and obtain a new equation:

1. **LS + A = RS + A,   LS - A = RS – A**   Add or Subtract a Number to both sides of the equation.
2. **LSxA = RSxA, LS÷A = RS÷A**   Multiply or Divide a Number
3. **1/LS = 1/RS**   Invert both sides
4. **(LS)^2 = (RS)^2**   Square both sides
5. **√LS = √RS**   Square Root Both Sides
6. SIN (**LS**) = SIN (**RS**)   Take the SIN of both sides.
7. Any legitimate math operation to both sides.

The idea is to apply a sequence of operations or transformations to both sides until you arrive at:

    X = Number   "The Solution"

Then **check your answer** by substituting this Number into the Equation in place of **X** and see that both sides are equal.
We will see many examples of this in the lessons to follow. These are the kinds of Equations you will be solving in the "real world."

THE RULE OF ALGEBRA

Suppose we have an equation to solve. It will have a Left Side (**LS**) and a Right Side (**RS**) either of which might contain the unknown, **X**, and other known numbers. (Any letter could be the unknown.)

Equation: **LS = RS** Can switch sides **RS = LS**

1. What is **THE RULE** of Equation Solving?

2. Give examples of applying this Rule.

3. Describe the process you will use to solve an equation using this Rule.

4. After you have a solution: **X** = Number, what should you always do, especially if the answer is important?

THE RULE OF ALGEBRA

Suppose we have an equation to solve. It will have a Left Side (**LS**) and a Right Side (**RS**) either of which might contain the unknown, **X**, and other known numbers. (Any letter could be the unknown.)

Equation: **LS = RS**   Can switch sides   **RS = LS**

1. **THE RULE** of Equation Solving is: *You may do the same thing to both sides of the equation and obtain a new equation:*

2. Examples:
1) **LS + A = RS + A,   LS - A = RS - A**   (add or subtract a number to both sides of the equation)
2) **LSxA = RSxA, LS÷A = RS÷A**   (multiply or divide a number)
3) **1/LS = 1/RS**   (invert both sides)
4) $(\mathbf{LS})^2 = (\mathbf{RS})^2$ (square both sides)
5) **√LS = √RS**   (square root both sides)
6) SIN (**LS**) = SIN (**RS**)   (take the SIN of both sides)
7) Any legitimate math operation to both sides.

3. The idea is to apply a sequence of operations or transformations to both sides until you arrive at:

     X = Number   "**The Solution**"

4. Then <u>check your answer</u> by substituting this Number into the Equation in place of X and see that both sides are equal.
We will see many examples of this in the lessons to follow. These are the kinds of Equations you will be solving in the "real world."

THE RULE OF ALGEBRA

1. When solving an equation, any math operation (adding, subtracting, multiplying, etc.) done to one side of the equation must be _____. *fill in the blank*

2. If we solved the equation X + 3 = 8, and got X = 6, what IMPORTANT STEP would help us realize we made a mistake?

THE RULE OF ALGEBRA   Answers: [ ]

1. When solving an equation, any math operation (adding, subtracting, multiplying, etc.) done to one side of the equation must be [done to the other side of the equation].

2. If we solved the equation X + 3 = 8, and got X = 6, what IMPORTANT STEP would help us realize we made a mistake?
   [If we checked our solution by plugging it back into the original equation we would see that X = 6 gives 9 = 8, which is obviously incorrect!]

A3 LESSON: X + A = B   THIS IS AN EASY LINEAR EQUATION

What can you do to both sides to get closer to a solution?

X + A - A = B - A   [subtract **A** from both sides] [transpose **A**]

Thus: X = B – A   since   **A - A = 0**   and   **X + 0 = X**

Example: X + 2 = 5   [subtract **2** from both sides]

Solution: X = X + 2 - 2 = 5 - 2 = 3

Example: X - 7 = -13   [add **7** to both sides]

Solution: X = X - 7 + 7 = -13 + 7 = -6   [we have transposed 7]

Example: 8.13 = -7.19 + X

Same as: X - 7.19 = 8.13   [since can switch sides]

Solution: Add 7.19 to both sides. X = 15.32 (use calculator)

Example: X + (-18.4) = +$\sqrt{37.9}$

Same as: X - 18.4 = 6.16   [take square root +(-) = -]
       X = X - 18.4 + 18.4 = 6.16 + 18.4 = 24.56 = 24.6

       [add 18.4]

Example: X - SIN(37°) = [COS(68°)]2 [do not be intimidated

       SIN(37°) = .6018 COS(68°) = .3746 $(.3746)^2$ = .1403

  SO: X - .6018 = .1403 and

  THUS: X = .7421

A3E

X + A = B   THIS IS AN EASY LINEAR EQUATION

X + A - A = B - A   [subtract A from both sides] [transpose A]

Thus: X = B – A   since A - A = 0   and X + 0 = X

Solve for X, the Unknown

1. X + 42 = 59

2. X - 17 = -43

3. 8.13 = -17.19 + X

4. X + (-28.4) = +$\sqrt{87.9}$

5. 6.5 - X = 23.5

6. 5,432 = X + 4,375

7. X - $\sqrt{675}$ = $\sqrt{9,876}$

8. X - 3/4 = 9/13

9. 6/7 = 8/11 – X

10. 0.00035 + X = 0.0017

11. X - $SIN(37^\circ)$ = $[COS(68^\circ)]^2$

12. $COS(48^\circ)$ = $TAN(78^\circ)$ – X

13. $(13.4 + 9.7)^2$ + X = 87.4^2

X + A = B   THIS IS AN EASY LINEAR EQUATION   Answers: [ ]

X + A - A = B - A   [subtract A from both sides]   [transpose A]

Thus: X = B – A   since A - A = 0 and X + 0 = X

1. X + 42 = 59   [17]
2. X - 17 = -43   [-26]
3. 8.13 = -17.19 + X   [25.32]
4. X + (-28.4) = +$\sqrt{87.9}$ [37.8]
5. 6.5 - X = 23.5   [-17]
6. 5432 = X + 4375   [1057]
7. X - $\sqrt{675}$ = $\sqrt{9876}$ [125.36]
8. X - 3/4 = 9/13   [75/52=1 23/52]
9. 6/7 = 8/11 – X   [-10/77]
10. 0.00035 + X = 0.0017   [0.00135]
11. X - SIN(37°) = [COS(68°)]^2 [0.742]
12. COS(48°) = TAN(78°) – X   [4.035]
13. (13.4 + 9.7)^2 + X = 87.4^2 [7105.15]

X + A = B   THIS IS AN EASY LINEAR EQUATION

1. X + 54 = 100

2. 8.7 - X = 4.9

3. X + (-0.567) = 3.14

4. X + $\sqrt{25}$ = 10

5. 17^2 - X = 100

6. X - SIN(30°) = 1

7. X - 5/6 = 4/5

8. 7/6 = 8/5 - X

9. 0.3017^4 + X = 0.0012^2

10. $[COS(180°)]^2$ - X = SIN(270°)

11. π - X = π/2

12. $(2^3 + X)$ - 4 = $(2^2 + 3^2)$

X + A = B   THIS IS AN EASY LINEAR EQUATION
Answers: [ ]

1. X + 54 = 100   **[X = 46]**
2. 8.7 - X = 4.9   **[X = 3.8]**
3. X + (-0.567) = 3.14   **[X = 3.707]**
4. X + $\sqrt{25}$ = 10   **[X = 5]**
5. 17^2 - X = 100   **[X = 189]**
6. X - SIN(30°) = 1   **[X = 1.5]**
7. X - 5/6 = 4/5   **[X = 1.633]**
8. 7/6 = 8/5 - X   **[X = 0.433]**
9. 0.3017^4 + X = 0.0012^2 **[X = -0.00828]**
10. $[COS(180°)]^2$ - X = SIN(270°)   **[X = 2]**
11. π - X = π/2   **[X = π/2]**
12. $(2^3 + X)$ - 4 = $(2^2 + 3^2)$ **[X = 9]**

A4 LESSON: AX = B   THIS IS AN EASY LINEAR EQUATION

What can you do to both sides to get closer to a solution?

$X = AX/A = B/A$ [divide both sides by A]   **Note:** $A/A = 1$

Example: $3X = 12$

Solution: $X = 3X/3 = 12/3 = 4$ [divide by **3** both sides always]

Example: $2.16X = -56.3$

Solution: $X = -56.3/2.16 = -26.0648 = -26.1$

Example: $-37.8 = -6.78X$

Solution: $-6.78X = -37.8$ [switch sides]

Then: $X = (-37.8)/(-6.78) = 5.6$ [divide by -6.78]

Example: $(3.85)^2 X = \sqrt{349}/ \mathbf{SIN}(79^0)$ [easy does it!]

$(3.85)^2 = 14.8$ $\sqrt{349} = 18.7$ **SIN** $(79^0) = .982$

So: $14.8X = 18.7/.982 = 19.0$ $X = 1.29$ [divide by 14.8]

Always simplify the numbers first, and then solve the equation. The calculator makes this easy. Also, always **CHECK** your answer by plugging it back into the equation and being sure both sides are equal.

$(3.85)^2 x1.29 = 19.1$ $\sqrt{349}/ \mathbf{SIN}(79^0) = 19.0$ [round off error]

AX = B   THIS IS AN EASY LINEAR EQUATION

What can you do to both sides to get closer to a solution?

$X = AX/A = B/A$ [divide both sides by A]   **Note**: $A/A = 1$

Solve for X, the Unknown

1. $4X = 12$

2. $2.16X = -56.3$

3. $-37.8 = -6.78X$

4. $0.003X = 0.15$

5. $(4/5)X = 7/9$

6. $(1+3)^2X = \sqrt{65}$

7. $(3.85)^2X = \sqrt{349}/ SIN(79^0)$ {Easy does it!}

8. $(1 + 2/3) = (7/12)X$

9. $2{,}345X = 9{,}876$

10. $54.5 = -87.7X$

11. $COS(32^0)X = 3SIN(32^0)$

12. $X = 3TAN(32^0)$

A4EA
AX = B   THIS IS AN EASY LINEAR EQUATION
Answers: [ ]

What can you do to both sides to get closer to a solution?

X = AX/A = B/A   [divide both sides by A]   **Note**: A/A = 1

Solve for **X**, the Unknown

1. 4X = 12   [3]
2. 2.16X = -56.3   [-26.1]
3. -37.8 = -6.78X   [5.58]
4. 0.003X = 0.15   [50]
5. (4/5)X = 7/9   [35/36 = 0.97]
6. $(1+3)^2$X = √65   [0.5]
7. $(3.85)^2$X =√349/ SIN(79^0) [1.28]
8. (1 + 2/3) = (7/12)X   [20/7 = 2 6/7 = 2.86]
9. 2,345X = 9,876   [4.2]
10. 54.5 = -87.7X   [-0.62]
11. COS(32^0)X = 3SIN(32^0)   [1.875]
12. X = 3TAN (32^0)   [1.875]

AX = B THIS IS AN EASY LINEAR EQUATION

1. $5X = 27.25$

2. $67 - 2 = 13X$

3. $5.1X - 3 = 2.1$

4. $9 = 3X + 17$

5. $(5^2)X = 1000$

6. $TAN(30°)X = 18$

7. $(\sqrt{169})X = 26$

8. $(-7/8) = (-8/5)X$

9. $[SIN(60°)]^2X = 3$

10. *In the equation AX = B, when solving it we would divide B by A. Notice how dividing B by A is the same as MULTIPLYING B by (1/A).* In the equation, (2/3)X = 2, we would solve by dividing 2 by (2/3). If we want to think in terms of multiplication, what we would multiply 2 by instead?

11. $(\sqrt{36})[COS(60°)]^2 = SIN(270°)X$

12. $3X + 3X + 3X = -0.62612$

AX = B   THIS IS AN EASY LINEAR EQUATION

Answers: [ ]

1. $5X = 27.25$ **[X = 5.45]**

2. $67 - 2 = 13X$ **[X = 5]**

3. $5.1X - 3 = 2.1$ **[X = 1]**

4. $9 = 3X + 17$ **[X = - 2.67]**

5. $(5^2)X = 1000$ **[X = 40]**

6. $TAN(30°)X = 18$ **[X = 31.18]**

7. $(\sqrt{169})X = 26$ **[X = 2]**

8. $(-7/8) = (-8/5)X$ **[X = 0.5469]**

9. $[SIN(60°)]^2X = 3$ **[X = 4]**

10. *In the equation AX = B, when solving it we would divide B by A. Notice how dividing B by A is the same as MULTIPLYING B by (1/A).* In the equation, (2/3)X = 2, we would solve by dividing 2 by (2/3). If we want to think in terms of multiplication, what we would multiply 2 by instead?

    [We would think of multiplying 2 by the reciprocal of 2/3, which is 3/2.]

11. $(\sqrt{36})[COS(60°)]^2 = SIN(270°)X$ **[X = -1.5]**

12. $3X + 3X + 3X = -0.62612$ **[X = -0.0696]**

A5 LESSON: AX+B = CX+D THIS IS AN EASY LINEAR EQUATION

What can you do to both sides to get closer to a solution?

Get all the X terms on one side and numbers on other side.

$AX - CX = D - B$ or $(A - C)X = D - B$ [distributive law]

$X = (D - B)/(A - C)$ [divide both sides by (A - C)]

Example: $3X + 7 = 5 - 7X$

Solution: $3X + 7X = 5 - 7$ **or** $10X = -2$ **or** $X = -2/10 = -.5$

Example: $-18.3X + 4.6X - 22.4 = 13.9X - 45.4 + 3.9X$

   $-18.3X + 4.6X - 13.9X - 3.9X = -45.4 + 22.4$

   $(-18.3 + 4.6 - 13.9 - 3.9)X = -31.5X = -23.0$

   $X = -23.0/-31.5 = .730$

Once again...always do the numerical calculations first.

Example: $(2.13)^2X - LOG(345) = 1/COS(12.5°) + \sqrt{(5 + 1/.15)}X$

   $(2.13)^2 = 4.54$ $LOG (345) = 2.54$

   $COS(12.5°) = .976$ $1/.976 = 1.024$

and: $\sqrt{(5 + 1/.15)} = \sqrt{(5 + 6.67)} = 3.42$ [easy w/calculator]

   $4.54X - 2.54 = 1.024 + 3.42X$

or: $(4.54 - 3.42)X = 1.024 + 2.54$

   $1.12X = 3.56$

   $X = 3.56/1.12 = 3.18$ [you check the answer]

   $(2.13)^2 x3.18 - LOG (345) = 11.9 = 1/COS (12.5°) +$

   $\sqrt{(5 + 1/.15)}3.18$

AX + B = CX + D   THIS IS AN EASY LINEAR EQUATION.

Solve for X, the Unknown. **Note:** The Algebra is easy. The arithmetic can be complicated but easy with the **TI-30XA**.

1. $3X + 7 = 5 - 7X$

2. $3.2X - 9 = 4.1X + 7.8$

3. $-12X - 98 = 23X + 76$

4. $0.002X - 0.015 = 0.0087 - 0.005X$

5. $(3/4)X - 2/7 = (4/5)X + 3/8$

6. $SIN(28^o)X - 1.4 = COS(28^o)X + 2.3$

7. $-18.3X + 4.6X - 22.4 = 13.9X - 45.4 + 3.9X$

8. $(2.13)^2X - LOG(345) = 1/COS(12.5^o) + \sqrt{(5 + 1/0.15)}\ X$

9. $2\ 5/6X - 7.1 = 7\ 2/3X + 3.2$

10. $(1/7)X + 2/3 = (3/8)X - 4/9$

11. $2.4 - 3.5X = 7.8 - 1.2X$

12. $(LOG54)X + 45^2 = SIN(45^o) - (4.5)^2X$

13. $X - LN(60) = 3 - 2X$

14. $45 - 17X = 8X + 76$

AX + B = CX + D This is an easy Linear Equation

Answers: [ ]

Solve for **X**, the **Unknown**. **Note:** The Algebra is easy. The arithmetic can be complicated but easy with the **TI-30XA**.

1. $3X + 7 = 5 - 7X$ [-0.2]

2. $3.2X - 9 = 4.1X + 7.8$ [-18.7]

3. $-12X - 98 = 23X + 76$ [-4.97]

4. $0.002X - 0.015 = 0.0087 - 0.005X$ [3.39]

5. $(3/4)X - 2/7 = (4/5)X + 3/8$ [-13 3/14 = -185/14 = -13.21]

6. $SIN(28^\circ)X - 1.4 = COS(28^\circ)X + 2.3$ [-8.95]

7. $-18.3X + 4.6X - 22.4 = 13.9X - 45.4 + 3.9X$ [0.73]

8. $(2.13)^2X - LOG(345) = 1/COS(12.5^\circ) + \sqrt{(5 + 1/.15)}X$ [3.18]

9. $2\ 5/6X - 7.1 = 7\ 2/3X + 3.2$ [-2.13]

10. $(1/7)X + 2/3 = (3/8)X - 4/9$ [4 92/117 = 560/117 = 4.79]

11. $2.4 - 3.5X = 7.8 - 1.2X$ [-2.35]

12. $(LOG54)X + 45^2 = SIN(45^\circ) - (4.5)^2X$ [-92.09]

13. $X - LN(60) = 3 - 2X$ [2.37]

14. $45 - 17X = 8X + 76$ [-1.24]

AX + B = CX + D This is an easy Linear Equation

1. $4x - 17 = -35 - 5X$

2. $25 + 3.5X = -25 + 7.5X$

3. $6^2X - 24 = 36 + 18X$

4. $0.375 + 4.25X = 1.525 - 8.125X$

5. $SIN(45°)X - 4 = 12 - COS(45°)X$

6. $(\sqrt{144})X - 2^4 = 3^3 + (\sqrt{36})X$

7. $LOG(15)X + 1 = LN(25) + 2X$

8. $1/COS(0°) -4X = -1/SIN(90°) + (3/4)X$

9. $\pi X - 2/3\pi = 3\pi X - 8/3\pi$ *HINT: What can be removed from both sides of the equation?*

10. $2TAN(45°)X + 2X - 0.375 = SIN(12.5°)X - \sqrt{0.025}$

11. $(1/4)^2X - 25.67 = 27X + 6.022$

12. $[LN(25-7.4)]^2X - 17 = 1/LOG(2) - 3COS(37°)X$

AX + B = CX + D This is an easy Linear Equation

Answers: [ ]

1. $4x - 17 = -35 - 5X$ [X = -2]

2. $25 + 3.5X = -25 + 7.5X$ [X = 12.5]

3. $6^2X - 24 = 36 + 18X$ [X = 3.333]

4. $0.375 + 4.25X = 1.525 - 8.125X$ [X = 0.0929]

5. $SIN(45°)X - 4 = 12 - COS(45°)X$ [X = 11.31]

6. $(\sqrt{144})X - 2^4 = 3^3 + (\sqrt{36})X$ [X = 7.167]

7. $LOG(15)X + 1 = LN(25) + 2X$ [X = -2.693]

8. $1/COS(0°) - 4X = -1/SIN(90°) + (3/4)X$ [X = 0.421]

9. $\pi X - 2/3\pi = 3\pi X - 8/3\pi$ *HINT: What can be removed from both sides of the equation?*

   [Since Pi is on either side of the equation, it can be removed.]   [X = 1]

10. $2TAN(45°)X + 2X - 0.375 = SIN(12.5°)X - \sqrt{0.025}$

    [X = 0.0573]

11. $(1/4)^2X - 25.67 = 27X + 6.022$ [X = -1.176]

12. $[LN(25-7.4)]^2X - 17 = 1/LOG(2) - 3COS(37°)X$

    [X = 1.19]

A6 LESSON: A/X = C/D   THIS IS AN EASY LINEAR EQUATION

What can you do to both sides to get closer to a solution?

Flip both sides: X/A = D/C   **then**   X = Ax(D/C)

Example: 3/X = 12/5

Solution: X/3 = 5/12   **then**   X = 3x(5/12) = 1.25

Example: 2.16/X = -56.3   **then**   X/2.16 = 1/-56.3

Solution: X = 2.16/-56.3 = -.038   (check: 2.16/-.038 = -56.8)

Example: -37.8 = -6.78/X

Solution: -6.78/X = -37.8   (switch sides)

  Then: X = (-6.78)/(-37.8) = .18   (flip and multiply by -6.78)

Example: $(3.85)^2$/X =√349/ **SIN**(79^0)

  $(3.85)^2$ = 14.8   √349 = 18.7   **SIN** (79^0) = .982

  So: 14.8/X = 18.7/.982 = 19.0   **or**   X = 14.8/19.0 = .78

Always simplify the numbers first, and then solve the equation.
Also, always **CHECK** your answer by plugging it back into the
equation and being sure both sides are equal.

  $(3.85)^2$/.78 = 19.0   √349/ **SIN**(79^0) = 19.0

A/X = C/D   THIS IS AN EASY LINEAR EQUATION.

Flip both sides: $X/A = D/C$ **then** $X = A \times (D/C)$

Solve for **X**, the **Unknown**. **Note:** The Algebra is easy. The arithmetic can be complicated but easy with the **TI-30XA**.

1. $3/X = 12/5$

2. $2.16/X = -56.3$

3. $-37.8 = -6.78/X$

4. $(3.85)^2/X = \sqrt{349}/ \textbf{SIN}(79^0)$

Always simplify the numbers first and then, solve the equation. Also, always **CHECK** your answer by plugging it back into the equation and being sure both sides are equal.

5. $\textbf{SIN}(23^0)/X = \textbf{COS}(54^0)$

6. $23^2 = (12.5)^2/X$

7. $(3/4)/X = 9/16$

8. $\textbf{LOG}(4235)/X = \text{LN } 435$

9. $10.5/X = 9.8/4.1$

10. $(5^2 + 7^2)/X = 1/(0.05)^2$

11. $\textbf{COS}(37^0)/\textbf{SIN}(37^0) = 1/X$

A/X = C/D This is an easy Linear Equation

Answers: [ ]

Flip both sides: $X/A = D/C$ **then** $X = A \times (D/C)$

Solve for **X**, the **Unknown**. **Note:** The Algebra is easy. The arithmetic can be complicated but easy with the **TI-30XA**.

1. $3/X = 12/5$ **[1.25]**

2. $2.16/X = -56.3$ **[-0.038]**

3. $-37.8 = -6.78/X$ **[0.179]**

4. $(3.85)^2/X = \sqrt{349}/ \text{SIN}(79^0)$ **[0.779]**

Always simplify the numbers first, and then solve the equation. Also, always **CHECK** your answer by plugging it back into the equation and being sure both sides are equal.

5. $\text{SIN}(23^0)/X = \text{COS}(54^0)$ **[0.665]**

6. $23^2 = (12.5)^2/X$ **[0.295]**

7. $(3/4)/X = 9/16$ **[1 1/3 = 4/3 = 1.33]**

8. **LOG**$(4235)/X = $ **LN** 435 **[0.597]**

9. $10.5/X = 9.8/4.1$ **[4.39]**

10. $(5^2 + 7^2)/X = 1/(0.05)^2$ **[0.185]**

11. **COS**$(37^0)/$**SIN**$(37^0) = 1/X$ **[0.754]**

A/X = C/D   This is an easy Linear Equation

1. $4/X = 1$

2. $10/X = 2/4$

3. $17/X = 1/17$

4. $SIN(30°)/X = 1/COS(60°)$

5. $25.3/X = -98.1/27.6$

6. $(\sqrt{225})/X = 12/19$

7. $23.6/-0.025 = 1112/X$

8. $SIN(56°)/X = COS(27°)$

9. $TAN(75°)/COS(23.5°) = SIN(14°)/X$

10. $LOG(92)/X = 15/LN(25)$

11. $\pi/X = 1/2$

12. $-COS(180°)/2X = 43SIN(25°)/3.643$

A/X = C/D   This is an easy Linear Equation

Answers: [ ]

1. $4/X = 1$ **[X = 4]**

2. $10/X = 2/4$ **[X = 20]**

3. $17/X = 1/17$ **[X = 289]**

4. $SIN(30°)/X = 1/COS(60°)$ **[X = 0.25]**

5. $25.3/X = -98.1/27.6$ **[X = -7.12]**

6. $(\sqrt{225})/X = 12/19$ **[X = 23.75]**

7. $23.6/-0.025 = 1112/X$ **[X = -1.178]**

8. $SIN(56°)/X = COS(27°)$ **[X = 0.93]**

9. $TAN(75°)/COS(23.5°) = SIN(14°)/X$ **[X = 0.0594]**

10. $LOG(92)/X = 15/LN(25)$ **[X = 0.4214]**

11. $π/X = 1/2$ **[X = 2π]**

12. $-COS(180°)/2X = 43SIN(25°)/3.643$ **[X = 0.1002]**

A7 LESSON: $AX^2 = B$ THIS IS AN EASY NON-LINEAR EQUATION

What can you do to both sides to get closer to a solution?

X^2 = B/A (divide by A) **now** take the square root both sides

$X = \sqrt{(B/A)}$ [**Note:** Answer could be **+** or **-**]

Example: X^2 = 387   X = 19.7 **or**   -19.7   [$\sqrt{387}$ = 19.7]

Example: $SIN(125^o)X^2 = (5.4 + 3.4)^2$ (simplify numbers first)

$SIN(125^o)$ = .819 $(5.4 + 3.4)^2 = (8.8)^2 = 77.4$

So: $.819X^2$ = 77.4 or X^2 = 77.4/.819 or X^2 = 94.55

So: X = 9.7

Check: $SIN(125^o) \times (9.7)^2$ = 77.07 [close enough due to **r/o**]

Note: $X = \sqrt{94.55}$ = 9.724 to more digits

Then: $SIN(125^o) \times (9.724)^2$ = 77.5

Always be aware of how many digits are really significant and the unavoidable round off (**r/o**) error. Ask yourself: How accurate or precise can I measure, or do I need to measure?

$AX^2 = B$ THIS IS AN EASY NON-LINEAR EQUATION

$X^2 = B/A$ (divide by A)   **now**   take the square root both sides

$X = \sqrt{(B/A)}$ [**Note:** Answer could be **+** or **-**]

Solve for **X**, the **Unknown**. **Note:** The Algebra is easy. The arithmetic can be complicated but easy with the **TI-30XA**.

1. $X^2 = 387$

2. $SIN(125°)X^2 = (5.4 + 3.4)^2$

3. $X^2 = 23^2$

4. $X^2 = (\sqrt{78})^2$

5. $X^2 = LOG(98)$

6. $SIN(34°) = COS(23°)X^2$

7. $(3/4)X^2 = 9/16$

8. $X^2 = 16A^2$

9. $X^2 = (SIN(78°))^2 + (COS(78°))^2$

10. $X^2 = COS^{-1}[(3^2 + 4^2 - 6^2)/2x3x4]$

11. $X^2 = \sqrt{81}$

$AX^2 = B$ THIS IS AN EASY NON-LINEAR EQUATION

Answers:[ ]

X^2 = B/A (divide by A)   **now**   take the square root both sides

$X = \sqrt{(B/A)}$ [**Note:** Answer could be **+** or **-**]

Solve for **X**, the **Unknown**. **Note:** The Algebra is easy. The arithmetic can be complicated but easy with the **TI-30XA**.

1. $X^2 = 387$ [**19.7**]

2. $SIN(125^\circ)X^2 = (5.4 + 3.4)^2$ [**9.7**]

3. $X^2 = 23^2$ [**23**]

4. $X^2 = (\sqrt{78})^2$ [**$\sqrt{78}$**]

5. $X^2 = LOG(98)$ [**1.41**]

6. $SIN(34^\circ) = COS(23^\circ)X^2$ [**0.779**]

7. $(3/4)X^2 = 9/16$ [**0.866**]

8. $X^2 = 16A^2$ [**4A**]

9. $X^2 = (SIN(78^\circ))^2 + (COS(78^\circ))^2$ [**1**]

10. $X^2 = COS^{-1}[(3^2 + 4^2 - 6^2)/2x3x4]$ [**10.8**]

11. $X^2 = \sqrt{81}$ [**3**]

$AX^2 = B$ THIS IS AN EASY NON-LINEAR EQUATION

1. $X^2 = 81$

2. $X^2 = 169$

3. $3X^2 = 45$

4. $X^2 = 275^2$

5. $SIN(35°)X^2 = 65$

6. $(3/7)X^2 = (19/8)$

7. $LOG(8.756)X^2 = LN(253)$

8. $X^2 = \pi^2$

9. $3X^2 = \sqrt{121}$

10. $X^2 = SIN(65°) - COS(45°)$

11. $4X^2 = (2^4 + 3^3 + 4^2)^2$

12. $X^2 = (3\pi^2)^2$

$AX^2 = B$ THIS IS AN EASY NON-LINEAR EQUATION

Answers:[ ]

1. $X^2 = 81$ [X = ±9]

2. $X^2 = 169$ [X = ±13]

3. $3X^2 = 45$ [X = ±3.87]

4. $X^2 = 275^2$ [X = ±275]

5. $SIN(35°)X^2 = 65$ [X = ±10.645]

6. $(3/7)X^2 = (19/8)$ [X = ±2.354]

7. $LOG(8.756)X^2 = LN(253)$ [X = ±2.423]

8. $X^2 = \pi^2$ [X = ±π]

9. $3X^2 = \sqrt{121}$ [X = ±1.915]

10. $X^2 = SIN(65°) - COS(45°)$ [X = ±0.4463]

11. $4X^2 = (2^4 + 3^3 + 4^2)^2$ [X = ±29.5]

12. $X^2 = (3\pi^2)^2$ [X = ±3π²]

Revised 2023-01-12

A8 LESSON: $A\sqrt{X} = B$ THIS IS AN EASY NON-LINEAR EQUATION

What can you do to both sides to get closer to a solution?

$\sqrt{X} = B/A$ (divide by A)   **now**   take the square both sides

$X = (B/A)^2$ [**Note:** Answer will be positive]

Example: $\sqrt{X} = 387$ $X = 149{,}769$ which is $(387)^2$

How many digits are significant...**probably 3.**
150,000 is good enough.

Example: $SIN(125^o)\sqrt{X} = (5.4 + 3.4)^2$ (simplify numbers first)
$SIN(125^o) = .819$ $(5.4 + 3.4)^2 = (8.8)^2 = 77.4$

So: $.819\sqrt{X} = 77.4$ **or** $\sqrt{X} = 77.4/.819$ **or** $\sqrt{X} = 94.55$

or $X = 8940$

Check: $SIN(125^o) \times \sqrt{8940} = 77.4$

Always be aware of how many digits are really significant and the unavoidable round off (**r/o**) error. Ask yourself: How accurate or precise can I measure, or do I need to measure?

A8E

$A\sqrt{X} = B$ This is an easy non-Linear Equation

$\sqrt{X} = B/A$ (divide by A)   **now**   take the square both sides

$X = (B/A)^2$ [**Note:** Answer will be positive]

Solve for **X**, the **Unknown**. **Note:** The Algebra is easy. The arithmetic can be complicated but is easy with the **TI-30XA**.

1. $\sqrt{X} = 387$

2. $\sqrt{X} = -23.5$

3. $\sqrt{X} = 7/8$

4. $3.5\sqrt{X} = 98.2$

5. $78 = 4.2\sqrt{X}$

6. $\sqrt{X} = 6^2$

7. $\sqrt{X} = \sqrt{17}$

8. $\mathbf{SIN}(125°)\sqrt{X} = (5.4 + 3.4)^2$ (simplify numbers first)

9. $\sqrt{X} = \mathbf{LOG}(6754)$

10. $\sqrt{X} = \mathbf{SIN}^2(65°) + \mathbf{COS}^2(65°)$

$A\sqrt{X} = B$ This is an easy non-Linear Equation

Answers:[ ]

$\sqrt{X} = B/A$ (divide by A)   now   take the square both sides

$X = (B/A)^2$ [**Note:** Answer will be positive]

Solve for **X**, the **Unknown**. **Note:** The Algebra is easy. The arithmetic can be complicated but easy with the **TI-30XA**.

1. $\sqrt{X} = 387$ [149,769]

2. $\sqrt{X} = -23.5$ [552.25]

3. $\sqrt{X} = 7/8$ [0.766 or 49/64]

4. $3.5\sqrt{X} = 98.2$ [787]

5. $78 = 4.2\sqrt{X}$ [345]

6. $\sqrt{X} = 6^2$ [1296]

7. $\sqrt{X} = \sqrt{17}$ [17]

8. $SIN(125°)\sqrt{X} = (5.4 + 3.4)^2$ [8937]

9. $\sqrt{X} = LOG(6754)$ [14.67]

10. $\sqrt{X} = SIN^2(65°) + COS^2(65°)$ [1]

$A\sqrt{X} = B$ This is an easy non-Linear Equation

1. $\sqrt{X} = 9$

2. $\sqrt{X} = 3/4$

3. $2.5\sqrt{X} = 10$

4. $\sqrt{X} = \cos(30°)$

5. $\sqrt{X} = \sqrt{225}$

6. $\sqrt{X} = \cos(75°)/\log(25)$

7. $\sqrt{X} = \cos(45°) + \sin(45°)$

8. $(\sqrt{X})^2 = (30.25)^2$

9. $\sqrt{X} = [\cos(12.5°) + \tan(12.5°)]/\sin(12.5°)$

10. $\sqrt{25}\sqrt{X} = 2000$

11. $\sqrt{(16X)} = 24$ *HINT: $\sqrt{(16X)} = \sqrt{16}\sqrt{X}$*

12. $\sin(87°)\sqrt{25X} = \log(63)$

A√X = B   This is an easy non-Linear Equation

Answers:[ ]

1. √X = 9   [X = 81]

2. √X = 3/4   [X = 9/16]

3. 2.5√X = 10   [X = 16]

4. √X = COS(30°)   [X = 0.75]

5. √X = √225   [X = 225]

6. √X = COS(75°)/LOG(25)   [X = 0.0343]

7. √X = COS(45°) + SIN(45°)   [X = 2]

8. (√X)² = (30.25)²   [X = 915.0625]

9. √X = [COS(12.5°) + TAN(12.5°)]/SIN(12.5°)

                                                        [X = 30.636]

10. √25√X = 2000   [X = 160,000]

11. √(16X) = 24 *HINT: √(16X) = √16√X*   [X = 36]

12. SIN(87°)√25X = LOG(63)   [X = 0.3604]

A9 LESSON: (1) SIN X^O = A, $-1 \leq A \leq 1$, OR (2) $SIN^{-1}X = A^O$, $0 \leq A^O \leq 180^O$

NOTE: Contrary to the audio, you cannot defer this lesson.

Two easy equations. (Apply correct **Inverse** to both sides)

Note: X is **angle** measured degrees (^{O}) in the first equation
   A is **angle** measured in degrees (^{O}) in the second equation

Note: You don't need to even know what **SIN** means to solve the equation using the calculator.

Example: **SIN** X^O = .548   Apply **SIN**$^{-1}$ to both sides
      X^O = **SIN**$^{-1}$(.548) = 33.2^O **Note:** 2nd **SIN** yields **SIN**$^{-1}$

Example: **SIN** X = .8765   X = 61.2^O [X is in ^{O}]

Example: **SIN**$^{-1}$X = 28° Apply **SIN** to both sides and get X = **SIN**(**SIN**$^{-1}$X) = **SIN**(28°) = .469

Example: (.75 + **COS**49°)**SIN**$^{-1}$X = (14.23 + **SIN**35°)^2
(Looks bad, but is really easy. Just do the numbers first.)

COS49^O = .656; **so** .75 + .656 = 1.41 **and**

SIN35^O = .574; **so** (14.23 + .574)^2 = 219 and so we get

1.41**SIN**$^{-1}$X = 219, **or** **SIN**$^{-1}$X = 219/1.41 = 155°

Thus, X = **SIN** 155° = .416

Check: 1.41x**SIN**$^{-1}$.416 = 1.41x24.6 = 34.7, not 219.

Something wrong. Must wait until **Trig Lesson T2** to understand.

Preview hint: **SIN**155° = **SIN** 25°

A9 (1) SIN X^o = A, -1 ≤ A ≤ 1, or (2) SIN-1X = A^o ,0 ≤ A^o≤ 180°

Two easy equations. (Apply correct **Inverse** to both sides)

Note: X is **angle** measured degrees (^{o}) in the first equation

A is **angle** measured in degrees (^{o}) in the second equation

Note: You don't need to even know what **SIN** means to solve the equation using the calculator.

Example: **SIN X^o = .548**   Apply **SIN^{-1}** to both sides

X^o = SIN^{-1}(.548) = 33.2^0 **Note:** 2nd **SIN** yields **SIN^{-1}**

Example: **SIN X = .8765**   X = 61.2^0 [X is in ^{o}]

Example: **SIN^{-1}X = 28^0**   Apply **SIN** to both sides and get X = SIN(SIN^{-1}X) = SIN(28^0) = .469

Example: (.75 + **COS**49°)**SIN^{-1}**X = (14.23 + SIN35^o)^2
(Looks bad, but is really easy. Just do the numbers first.)

COS49^o = .656   **so**   .75 + .656 = 1.41 **and**

SIN35^o = .574   **so**   (14.23 + .574)^2 = 219 and so we get

1.41**SIN^{-1}**X = 219, or **SIN^{-1}**X = 219/1.41 = 155°

Thus,   X = SIN 155^0 = .416

Check: 1.41x**SIN^{-1}**.416 = 1.41x24.6 = 34.7, not 219.

Something wrong. Must wait until Trig **Lesson T2** to understand.

Preview hint: **SIN**155° = **SIN** 25°

$$(1) \ SIN \ X^\circ = A, \ -1 \le A \le 1, \ or$$

$$(2) \ SIN^{-1}X = A^\circ, \ 0 \le A^\circ \le 180^\circ$$

Two easy equations. (Apply correct **Inverse** to both sides)

Note: X is angle measured degrees ($^\circ$) in the first equation
    A is **angle** measured in degrees ($^\circ$) in the second equation

Solve for X, the Unknown. **Note:** The Algebra is easy. The arithmetic can be complicated, but is easy with the **TI-30XA**.

1. $SIN \ X^\circ = 0.548$

2. $SIN \ X^\circ = 0.8765,$

3. $SIN^{-1}X = 28^\circ$

4. $2.3SIN \ X^\circ = 1.92$

5. $SIN \ X^\circ = 1.5$

6. $SIN^{-1}(0.8765) = X^\circ$

7. $SIN^{-1}(SIN(56^\circ) = X$

8. $SIN(SIN^{-1}(0.321) = X$

9. $SIN^{-1}(X^2) = 15^\circ$

10. $SIN(3X^\circ) = 0.5$

$$(1)\ SIN\ X° = A,\ -1 \le A \le 1,\ or$$

$$(2)\ SIN^{-1}X = A°,\ 0 \le A° \le 180°$$

Answers: [ ]

Two easy equations. (Apply correct **Inverse** to both sides)

Note: X is angle measured degrees (°) in the first equation
   A is **angle** measured in degrees (°) in the second equation

Solve for **X**, the **Unknown**. Note; The Algebra is easy. The arithmetic can be complicated, but easy with the **TI-30XA**.

1. SIN X° = 0.548   [**33.23°**]

2. SIN X° = 0.8765   [**61.22°**]

3. $SIN^{-1}X = 28°$ [**0.4695**]

4. 2.3SIN X° = 1.92   [**56.6°**]

5. SIN X° = 1.5   [No Solution, Impossible]

6. $SIN^{-1}(0.8765) = X°$ [61.22°]

7. $SIN^{-1}(SIN(56°) = X$ [**56°**]

8. $SIN(SIN^{-1}(0.321) = X$ [0.321]

9. $SIN^{-1}(X^2) = 15°$ [0.5087]

10. SIN(3X°) = 0.5   [10°]

$$\text{(1) SIN } X^{o} = A, -1 \le A \le 1, \text{ or}$$

$$\text{(2) SIN}^{-1}X = A^{o}, 0 \le A^{o} \le 180^{o}$$

1. $SIN\ X° = 0.765$
2. $SIN\ X° = 0.278$
3. $SIN^{-1}(0.254) = X°$
4. $SIN^{-1}(X) = 45°$
5. $SIN\ X° = 2.89$
6. $SIN(SIN^{-1}(0.5)) = X$
7. $SIN(125°) = X$
8. $64SIN(X°) = 38.99$
9. $SIN(SIN^{-1}(0.75)) = X$
10. $SIN^{-1}(COS(60°)) = X°$
11. $SIN(X°^{2}) = 0.171$
12. $SIN^{-1}(COS(115))=X$

$$(1)\ SIN\ X^0 = A,\ -1 \le A \le 1,\ or$$

$$(2)\ SIN^{-1}X = A^0,\ 0 \le A^0 \le 180^0$$

Answers: [ ]

1. $SIN\ X° = 0.765$ [X = 49.9°]

2. $SIN\ X° = 0.278$ [X = 16.14°]

3. $SIN^{-1}(0.254) = X°$ [X = 14.71°]

4. $SIN^{-1}(X) = 45°$ [X = 0.707]

5. $SIN\ X° = 2.89$ [NO Solution]

6. $SIN(SIN^{-1}(0.5)) = X$ [X = 0.5]

7. $SIN(125°) = X$ [X = 0.8191]

8. $64SIN(X°) = 38.99$ [X = 37.53°]

9. $SIN(SIN^{-1}(0.75)) = X$ [X = 0.75]

10. $SIN^{-1}(COS(60°)) = X°$ [X = 30°]

11. $SIN(X°^2) = 0.171$ [X = ± 3.14°]

12. $SIN^{-1}(COS(115)) = X$ [X = -25]

A10 LESSON: (1) COS X° = A, -1 ≤ A ≤ 1, OR (2) $COS^{-1}X$ = A°, 0≤A≤180°

Two easy equations. (Apply **Inverse** to both sides)

Note: X is **angle** measured degrees ($^\circ$) first equation and
A is **angle** measured in degrees ($^\circ$) in second equation

Note: You don't need to even know what **COS** means to solve the equation using the calculator.

Example: COS X° = .548   Apply COS^{-1} to both sides
X° = COS^{-1}(.548) = 56.7° [X was understood to be in $^\circ$] **Note:** 2nd **COS** yields COS^{-1}

Example: $COS^{-1}X$ = 28° Apply **COS** to both sides
X = COS($COS^{-1}X$) = COS(28°) = .883

Example: (.75 + **COS**49°)$COS^{-1}X$ = (14.23 + **SIN**35°)^2
(Looks bad, but is really easy. Just do the numbers first.)

COS49° = .656 **so** .75 + .656 = 1.41 **and**
SIN35° = .574 **so** (14.23 + .574)^2 = 219

So we have: 1.41$COS^{-1}X$ = 219 **or** $COS^{-1}X$ = 219/1.41 = 155
Thus: X = COS155° = -.906

Check: 1.41xCOS^{-1}(-.906) = 1.41x155 = 219

Note: We didn't have the same problem we had with the **SIN**. Why not? Have to wait until **Trig Lesson T3** for explanation.

A10E

$$(1) \; COS \; X^o = A, \; -1 \leq A \leq 1, \; or$$

$$(2) \; COS^{-1}X = A^o, \; 0 \leq A \leq 180^o$$

Two easy equations. (Apply **Inverse** to both sides)

Note: X is **angle** measured degrees (o) first equation and

A is angle measured in degrees (o) in second equation

Solve for **X**, the **Unknown**. **Note**: The Algebra is easy. The arithmetic can be complicated, but easy with the **TI-30XA.**

1. $COS \; X^o = 0.548$

2. $COS^{-1}X = 28^o$

3. $COS \; X^o = 0.982$

4. $COS \; X^o = SIN \; 79^o$

5. $COS^{-1}X = SIN^{-1}(0.435)$

6. $4COS(3X^o) = 2.56$

7. $2.3COS^{-1}(SIN \; X^o) = 45^o$

8. $(0.75 + COS49^o)COS^{-1}X = (14.23 + SIN35^o)^2$

9. $SIN^{-1}(SIN(125^o) = X^o$

10. $COS^{-1}(COS(125^o) = X^o$

A10EA

$$(1)\ COS\ X^O = A,\ -1 \le A \le 1,\ OR$$

$$(2)\ COS^{-1}X = A^O,\ 0 \le A \le 180^O$$

Answers: []

Two easy equations. (Apply Inverse to both sides)

Note: X is **angle** measured degrees (^{O}) first equation and
A is angle measured in degrees (^{O}) in second equation

Solve for X, the **Unknown**. **Note**: The Algebra is easy. The arithmetic can be complicated, but easy with the **TI-30XA**.

1. $COS\ X^O = 0.548$ [56.8^O]

2. $COS^{-1}X = 28^O$ [0.8829]

3. $COS\ X^O = 0.982$ [10.9^O]

4. $COS\ X^O = SIN\ 79^O$ [11°]

5. $COS^{-1}X = SIN^{-1}(0.435)$ [0.9004]

6. $4COS(3X^O) = 2.56$ [16.7^O]

7. $2.3COS^{-1}(SIN\ X^O) = 45^O$ [70.4^O]

8. $(0.75 + COS49^O)COS^{-1}X = (14.23 + SIN35^O)^2$
                                     [-0.9125]

9. $SIN^{-1}(SIN(125^O) = X^O$ [55°]

10. $COS^{-1}(COS(125^O) = X^O$ [125°]

$$(1)\ \text{COS } X^O = A,\ -1 \le A \le 1,\ \text{OR}$$

$$(2)\ \text{COS}^{-1}X = A^O,\ 0 \le A \le 180^O$$

1. COS X° = 0.267

2. COS X° = 0.6565

3. $\text{COS}^{-1}(0.125) = X°$

4. $\text{COS}^{-1}(X) = 45°$

5. COS X° = -0.725

6. COS X° = -1.76

7. -3.75COS(11°) = X

8. $\text{COS}^{-1}(X) = 115°$

9. $\text{COS}^{-1}(\text{SIN}(48°)) = X°$

10. COS (3X°) = -0.49

11. $\text{COS}^{-1}(X/3) = 75°$

12. SIN(16.5°)COS(X°) = 0.119

$$(1)\ \cos X^O = A,\ -1 \le A \le 1,\ OR$$

$$(2)\ \cos^{-1}X = A^O,\ 0 \le A \le 180^O$$

Answers: [ ]

1. $\cos X° = 0.267$ [X = 74.5°]

2. $\cos X° = 0.6565$ [X = 48.97°]

3. $\cos^{-1}(0.125) = X°$ [X = 82.82°]

4. $\cos^{-1}(X) = 45°$ [X = 0.707]

5. $\cos X° = -0.725$ [X = 136.47°]

6. $\cos X° = -1.76$ [NO solution]

7. $-3.75\cos(11°) = X$ [X = -3.681]

8. $\cos^{-1}(X) = 115°$ [X = -0.4226]

9. $\cos^{-1}(\sin(48°)) = X°$ [X = 42°]

10. $\cos(3X°) = -0.49$ [X = 39.78°]

11. $\cos^{-1}(X/3) = 75°$ [X = 0.7765]

12. $\sin(16.5°)\cos(X°) = 0.119$ [X = 65.23°]

INTRODUCTION TO GEOMETRY

The Foundation Course is dedicated to your learning how to solve practical math problems that arise in a wide variety of industrial and "real world" situations.

In addition to learning how to use the power tool called a scientific calculator, you need to learn material from three fields, Algebra, Geometry and Trigonometry.

Geometry is the "Centerpiece" of math that you will use in most problems. It is all about physical space in one, two, and three dimensions: Lines, Flat Surfaces and 3-D objects.

Algebra is a tool that is often used along with Geometry to solve problems.

You use Geometry to set up an equation which you then solve for the unknown. The unknown might be a length, or some dimension you need to know, or area, or volume.

Trigonometry is a special subject used for triangles. There are occasions where you cannot solve a problem with just algebra and geometry alone and where you need trigonometry. It deals with triangles.

Geometry is one of humankind's oldest mathematical subjects along with numbers and algebra.

Geometry is the foundation of modern science and technology and much modern mathematics.

Mathematics is like a "contact" sport, or a game.

You learn by practicing and "doing."

Each Lesson will include a video discussion of the topic just as we did in Algebra.

Then you will be given Homework Problems to work.

You are encouraged to make up your own problems.

The more you "play" and the more questions you ask, the better you will learn.

When you think you are ready, take the Online Quiz.

This will give you an indicator if you have mastered the material. If not, go back and "play" some more.

Learning math is like climbing a ladder. If you do it one small step at a time, it is pretty easy. But, it is difficult to go from rung 4 to rung 9 directly.

This Foundation course has been designed to let you climb the ladder of math understanding in small steps.

But, **YOU** must do the climbing. Watching someone else climb isn't enough. Play the game.

G1 LESSON: WHAT IS GEOMETRY?

Mathematics is based on two fundamental concepts:

Numbers and Geometry

Numbers are used to count and measure things.

Geometry is used to model physical things.

There are actually several different kinds of geometry.

We will study the oldest of all geometries, **Euclidean**.

Euclidean Geometry is used in most practical situations.

We will study:

Points:	0 dimensional
Lines:	1 dimensional
Surface Objects:	2 dimensions
And:	3-D objects

We will learn how to analyze many geometric situations and then set up **Equations** to find the value of various unknowns. This could be how long something is, or how much area something is, or the volume of something.

Many of the practical problems one comes across in many walks of life involve some type of geometric object.

Historically, in our schools, emphasis has been placed on proving theorems (statements about geometric objects) with rigorous logic and step by step deductions.

This can be difficult and tedious, and sometimes seemingly meaningless. We will emphasis sound reasoning in the Foundation Course, but not formal "proofs."

WHAT IS GEOMETRY?

1. Math is based on what two fundamental concepts?

2. Numbers are used to?

3. **Geometry** is used to?

4. The oldest kind of **Geometry** is?

5. In **Geometry** we will study what four things?

6. What will we use to find unknowns in **Geometry**?

7. What kind of **Unknowns** might we wish to find?

WHAT IS GEOMETRY?   Answers: []

1. Math is based on what two fundamental concepts?

    [**Numbers and Geometry**]

2. Numbers are used to?   [**Count and measure things**]

3. Geometry is used to?   [**Model physical things**]

4. The oldest kind of geometry is?   [**Euclidean**]

5. In Geometry we will study what four things?

    [**Points: 0 dimensional**]
    [**Lines: 1 dimension**]
    [**Surface Objects: 2 dimensions**]
    [**And: 3-D objects**]

6. What will we use to find Unknowns in Geometry?

    [**Equations and Algebra**]

7. What kind of Unknowns might we wish to find?

[**This could be how long something is, or how much area
    something is, or the volume of something.**]

Many of the practical problems one comes across in many walks
of life involve some type of geometric object.

Triad Math, Inc. © 2023
Revised 2023-01-12

G2 LESSON: STRAIGHT LINES AND ANGLES

A **Point** is ideally a location in space with no length or width. It has zero area.

A **Plane** is a flat surface consisting of points. Think of a wall or blackboard as a plane. It is a surface with zero curvature.

A **Straight Line** (Segment) is the collection of points between two points that represents the shortest distance between them. It too has zero curvature. A **Straight Line** can be extended indefinitely.

The intersection of two lines (**straight**, unless I otherwise state), forms an **Angle** and their point of intersection is called the **Vertex**.

Angles are measured in **Degrees** (°) where there are 360° in a complete circle, a set of points equidistant from a point, center.

A **Right Angle** measures 90° and the two sides are **Perpendicular**.

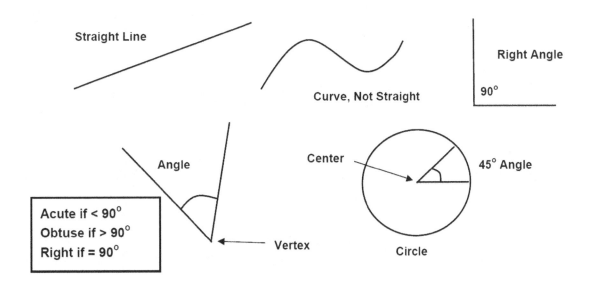

STRAIGHT LINES AND ANGLES

1. What are: Point, Plane, and Straight Line?

2. What are an Angle and a Vertex?

3. How are Angles measured?

4. What is a Right Angle?

5. What are Acute and Obtuse Angles?

STRAIGHT LINES AND ANGLES   Answers: []

1. What are: Point, Plane, and Straight Line?

    [A Point is ideally a location in space with no length or width. It has zero area.

    A Plane is a flat surface consisting of points. Think of a wall or blackboard as a plane. It is a surface with zero curvature.

    A Straight Line (Segment) is the collection of points between two points that represents the shortest distance between them.]

2. What are an Angle and a Vertex?

    [The intersection of two lines (straight, unless I otherwise state), forms an Angle and their point of intersection is called the Vertex.]

3. How are Angles measured?

    [Angles are measured in Degrees (^{o}) where there are 360° in a complete circle, a set of points equidistant from a point, center.]

4. What is a Right Angle?   [See Below Right]

5. What are Acute and Obtuse Angles? [See Below Left]

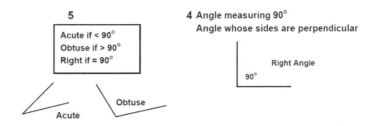

5

Acute if < 90°
Obtuse if > 90°
Right if = 90°

Acute

Obtuse

4 Angle measuring 90°
Angle whose sides are perpendicular

Right Angle

90°

G3 LESSON: PARALLEL LINES

Two straight lines are **parallel** if they never intersect no matter how far they are extended in either direction.

The Fundamental Property in **Euclidean** Geometry is:

Given a straight line and an external point, there is exactly one straight line through this point parallel to the given line.

This is called the **Parallel Postulate** and it is not true for other **non-Euclidean** geometries.

When two parallel lines are crossed by another straight line, called a **transversal**, eight angles are created in two sets of four equal-sized angles. This is a critical property.

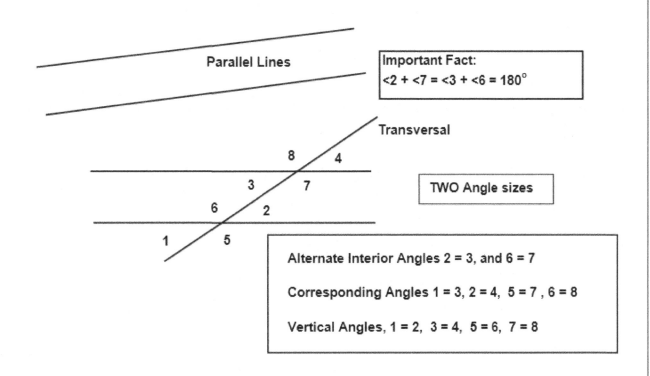

Parallel Lines

Important Fact:
$<2 + <7 = <3 + <6 = 180°$

Transversal

TWO Angle sizes

Alternate Interior Angles 2 = 3, and 6 = 7

Corresponding Angles 1 = 3, 2 = 4, 5 = 7, 6 = 8

Vertical Angles, 1 = 2, 3 = 4, 5 = 6, 7 = 8

G3 Problems for Parallel Lines

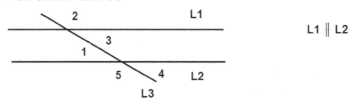

1. Given <1=42°, what are the sizes of <2 and <3?

2. Given <3=50°, what are the sizes of <4 and <5?

3. Given <2=132°, what are the sizes of <1 and <4?

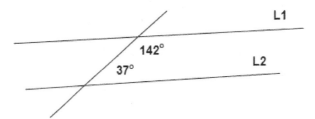

4. Are L1 and L2 parallel?

5. What is the sum of two interior angles if the lines are parallel?

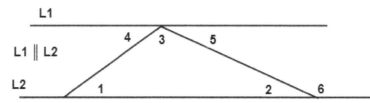

6. What is <4 + <3 +<5 =?

7. Which of the angles are equal <1, <2, <3, <4, <5=?

8. What is <1 + <2 + <3=?

9. If <1 = 43° and <3 = 102° then what does <6=?

10. In problem #9, what does <2=?

ANSWERS

1. <2 = 138° and <3 = 42°
2. <4 = 50° and <5 = 130°
3. <1 = <4 = 48°
4. No
5. 180°

6. 180°
7. <1 = <4 and <2 = <5
8. 180°
9. 43° + 102° = 145°
10. 180° -145° = 35°

PARALLEL LINES

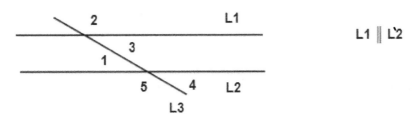

L1 ∥ L'2

1. Given <1 = 38°, what are the sizes of <2 and <3?

2. Given <3 = 54°, what are sizes of <4 and <5?

3. Given <2 = 138°, what are sizes of <1 and <5?

4. Given:

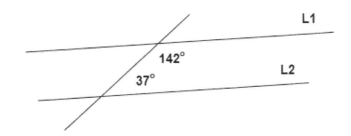

   Are L1 and L2 Parallel?

5. What is the sum of two opposite interior angles if the lines are parallel?

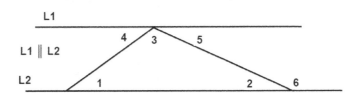

6. What is <4 + <3 + <5 =?

7. Which of these angles are equal <1, <2, <3, <4, <5?

8. What is <1 + <2 + <3 =?

9. If <1 = 42° and <3 = 105°, what does <6 =?

10. In problem #9, what does <2 =?

11. The sum of the three angles of a triangle equal?

PARALLEL LINES   Answers: []

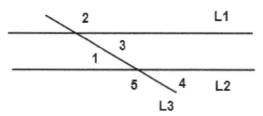

L1 ∥ L2

1. Given <1 = 38°, what are the sizes of <2 and <3?

    [<2 = 142° and <3 = 38°]

2. Given <3 = 54°, what are sizes of <4 and <5?

    [<4 = 54° and <5 = 126°]

3. Given <2 = 138°, what are sizes of <1 and <5?

    [<1 = 42° and <5 = 138°]

4. Given:

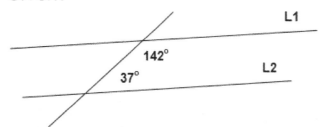

    Are L1 and L2 Parallel? [NO because: 142 + 37 = 179 not 80]

5. What is the sum of two interior angles if the lines are parallel?

    [<5 + <6 = 180°]

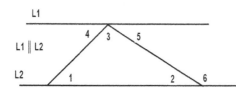

6. What is <4 + <3 + <5 =?   [180°]

7. Which of these angles are equal <1, <2, <3, <4, <5?

    [<1 = <4, <2 = <5]

PARALLEL LINES (cont'd)   Answers: []

8. What is <1 + <2 + <3 =?   [180°]

9. If <1 = 42° and <3 = 105°, what does <6 =?   [147°]

10. In problem #9, what does <2 =?   [33°]

11. The sum of the three angles of a triangle equal?   [180°]

PARALLEL LINES

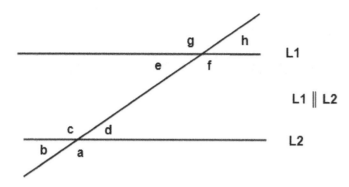

L1

L1 ‖ L2

L2

1.) How many angles do you need to know in order to replace the letters in the diagram to the left?

2.) If <a = 115, find the rest of the remaining angles.

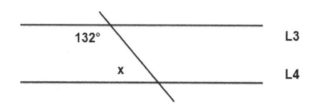

L3

L4

3.) If L3 and L4 are parallel, what must <x equal?

4.) If two lines are truly parallel, what will they never do?
Hint: Think about intersecting lines

PARALLEL LINES

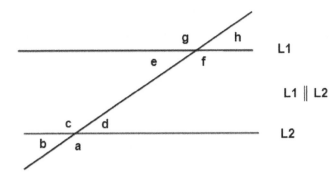

L1

L1 ‖ L2

L2

1.) How many angles do you need to know in order to replace the letters in the diagram to the left?

Answer: Only 1 angle.

2.) If <a = 115, find the rest of the remaining angles.

Answer: <b = <d = <e = <h = 65°, <a = <c = <f = <g = 115°

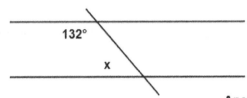

L3

L4

3.) If L3 and L4 are parallel, what must <x equal?

Answer: If L3 and L4 are parallel, <x and 132° must add up to 180°, therefore <x = 180 - 132 = 48°

4.) If two lines are truly parallel, what will they never do?
   Hint: Think about intersecting lines

Answer: Two parallel lines will never touch.

G4 LESSON: TRIANGLES, DEFINITION, SUM OF ANGLES

A Triangle is a three-sided **polygon**, i.e., a geometric figure created by three intersecting straight lines. Thus, a triangle has three sides and three vertices.

The sum of the three interior angles of a triangle is always 180°.
Exterior Angle = Sum of opposite Interiors

$1 + 2 + 3 = 180^o$ and $4 = 1 + 3$

Triangles are often used to model a physical situation.

There are several types of triangles:

Right, Acute, Obtuse, Isosceles, and Equilateral. See below.

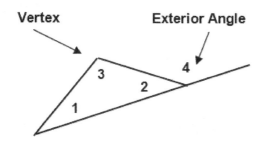

Vertex   **Exterior Angle**

<1 + <2 + <3 = 180o

<4 = <1 + <3

Acute   All angles < 90°

Obtuse   One angle > 90°

Right   One angle = 90°

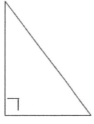

Right Triangle

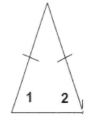

Isosceles Triangle
<1 = <2
Two Equal Sides

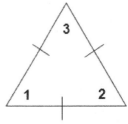

Equilateral Triangle
<1 = <2 = <3 = 60°

Three Equal Sides

G4 Triangle Problems

Finding unknown angles from known angles.

Each **vertex** of a triangle has four angles associated with it for a total of twelve angles for a triangle. There will be six values.

If you know any two angles from two different vertices, then you can calculate all the other angles.

This is demonstrated below.

Note 1: Angles do not have the < symbol

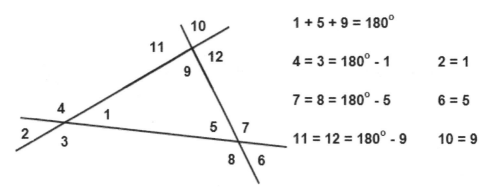

$$1 + 5 + 9 = 180^\circ$$

$$4 = 3 = 180^\circ - 1 \qquad 2 = 1$$

$$7 = 8 = 180^\circ - 5 \qquad 6 = 5$$

$$11 = 12 = 180^\circ - 9 \qquad 10 = 9$$

Given any two angles from two vertices, we can calculate all the other angles.

Example 1 $1 = 40^\circ$ and $7 = 120^\circ$ **Find the other angles**

Answers $5 = 6 = 180^\circ - 120^\circ = 60^\circ$ $8 = 120^\circ$

                 $4 = 3 = 180^\circ - 40^\circ$ $2 = 40^\circ$

    ** $9 = 10 = 180^\circ - 1 - 5 = 180^\circ - 40^\circ - 60^\circ = 80^\circ$

                 $11 = 12 = 180^\circ - 80^\circ = 100^\circ$

Example 2 $9 = 75^\circ$ and $8 = 110^\circ$ Find other angles

Answers $5 = 6 = 180^\circ - 110^\circ = 70^\circ$ and $7 = 110^\circ$

                 $11 = 12 = 180^\circ - 75^\circ = 105^\circ$ and $10 = 75^\circ$

    ** $2 = 1 = 180^\circ - 75^\circ - 70^\circ = 35^\circ$ and $4 = 3 = 180^\circ - 35^\circ = 145^\circ$

TRIANGLES

Find the unknown angles from known angles below.

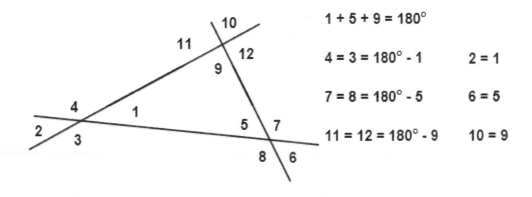

$$1 + 5 + 9 = 180°$$

$$4 = 3 = 180° - 1 \qquad 2 = 1$$

$$7 = 8 = 180° - 5 \qquad 6 = 5$$

$$11 = 12 = 180° - 9 \qquad 10 = 9$$

Given any two angles from two vertices, we can calculate all the other angles.

Exercise 1: $1 = 63°$ and $7 = 95°$ Find the other angles.

Exercise 2: $9 = 90°$ and $8 = 137°$ Find the other angles.

Exercise 3: $2 = 38°$ and $10 = 70°$ Find the other angles.

Exercise 4: $9 = 72°$ and $6 = 68°$ Find the other angles.

Exercise 5: $4 = 135°$ and $7 = 118°$ Find the other angles.

Exercise 6: $10 = 85°$ and $12 = 95°$ Find the other angles.

TRIANGLES

Find the unknown angles from known angles below.

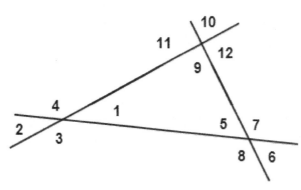

$1 + 5 + 9 = 180°$

$4 = 3 = 180° - 1$ $2 = 1$

$7 = 8 = 180° - 5$ $6 = 5$

$11 = 12 = 180° - 9$ $10 = 9$

Given any two angles from two vertices, we can calculate all the other angles.

Exercise 1
Answers

$1 = 63°$ and $7 = 95°$ Find the other angles
$5 = 6 = 180° - 95° = 85°$ $8 = 95°$
$4 = 3 = 180° - 63° = 117°$ $2 = 63°$
$11 = 12 = 180° - 32° = 148°$ $9 = 10 = 32°$

Exercise 2
Answers

$9 = 90°$ and $8 = 137°$ Find other angles
$5 = 6 = 180° - 37° = 43°$ and $7 = 137°$
$11 = 12 = 180° - 90° = 90°$ and $10 = 90°$
$2 = 1 = 180° - 90° - 43° = 47°$ and $4 = 3 = 180° - 47° = 133°$

Exercise 3
Answers

$2 = 38°$ and $10 = 70°$ Find the other angles
$1 = 38°$ and $3 = 4 = 142°$
$9 = 70°$ and $11 = 12 = 110°$
$5 = 6 = 72°$ and $7 = 8 = 108°$

Exercise 4
Answers

$9 = 72°$ and $6 = 68°$ Find the other angles
$5 = 6 = 68°$ and $7 = 8 = 112°$
$11 = 12 = 108°$ and $10 = 72°$
$2 = 1 = 40°$ and $4 = 3 = 140°$

Exercise 5
Answers

$4 = 135°$ and $7 = 118°$ Find the other angles
$5 = 6 = 62°$ and $7 = 8 = 118°$
$11 = 12 = 107°$ and $9 = 10 = 73°$
$2 = 1 = 45°$ and $4 = 3 = 135°$

Exercise 6
Answers

$10 = 85°$ and $12 = 95°$ Find the other angles
$9 = 85°$ and $11 = 95°$
Not enough information for the other angles.

TRIANGLES

Note: The interior angles of any polygon add up to the number of sides the shape has - 2 and then multiplied by 180.

Ex. Triangles have 3 sides --> (3 - 2) times 180 = 180°
Ex. Rectangles have 4 sides --> (4 - 2) times 180 = 360°

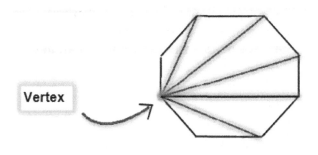

Vertex

1.) The reasoning behind this trick all comes back to triangles. How many degrees does a triangle's interior angles add up to?

2.) Now how many triangles can we break up this octagon into from a single vertex?

Note: A vertex is just a corner made by two lines!

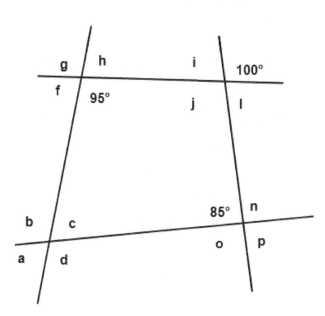

3.) With the help of this trick, find the remaining angles in the diagram to the left.

TRIANGLES

Note: The interior angles of any polygon add up to the number of sides the shape has - 2 and then multiplied by 180.

Ex. Triangles have 3 sides --> (3 - 2) times 180 = 180°
Ex. Rectangles have 4 sides --> (4 - 2) times 180 = 360°

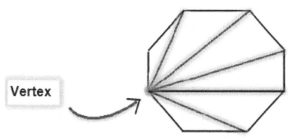

Vertex

1.) The reasoning behind this trick all comes back to triangles. How many degrees does a triangle's interior angles add up to?

Answer: 180°

2.) Now how many triangles can we break up this octagon into from a single vertex?

Note: A vertex is just a corner made by two lines!

Answer: 6 triangles

3.) With the help of this trick, find the remaining angles in the diagram to the left.

Answer:
a = c = 80°
b = d = 100°
f = h = 85°
g = 95°
i = l = 80°
j = 100°
n = o = 95°
p = 85°

The diagram to the left shows angles labeled g, h, i, 100°, f, 95°, j, l, b, c, 85°, n, o, p, a, d.

A **Right Triangle** has one of its angles = 90°

The side opposite the **right angle** is called the **Hypotenuse**.

The sum of the **other two angles** will sum to 90°

The Lengths of the three sides of a **Right Triangle** are related by the **Pythagorean Theorem**.

If, they are **a**, **b**, and **c** where "**c**" is the **hypotenuse**, then:

$$a^2 + b^2 = c^2$$

So, $c = \sqrt{a^2 + b^2}$; $b = \sqrt{c^2 - a^2}$; $a = \sqrt{c^2 - b^2}$

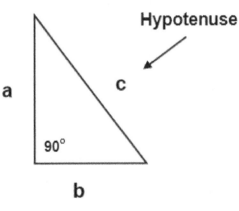

Hypotenuse

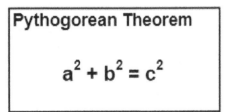

Pythogorean Theorem

$$a^2 + b^2 = c^2$$

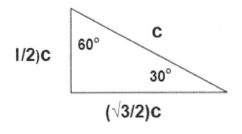

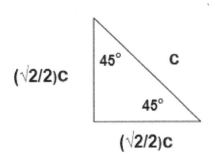

Typically, you are given one or two sides or angles and want to figure out the other sides or angles.

Here are a few examples (You will typically use the **Pythagorean Theorem** and a calculator):

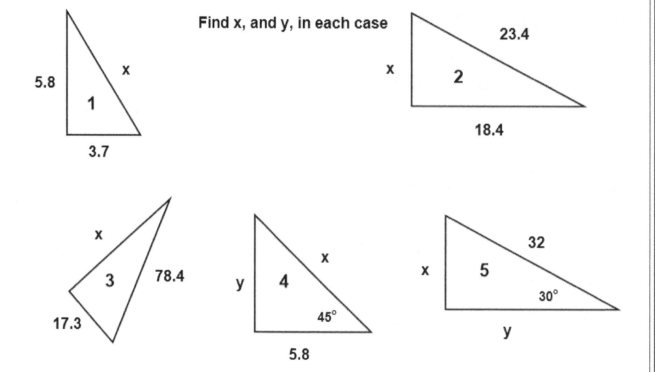

Find x, and y, in each case

Answers 1. x = 6.9 2. x = 14.5 3. 76.5 4. y = 5.8, x = 8.2 5. x = 16, y = 27.7

RIGHT TRIANGLES

Find **x** and **y** in each of the Exercises below.

You will typically use the **Pythagorean Theorem** and a calculator.

All triangles below are **right triangles**.

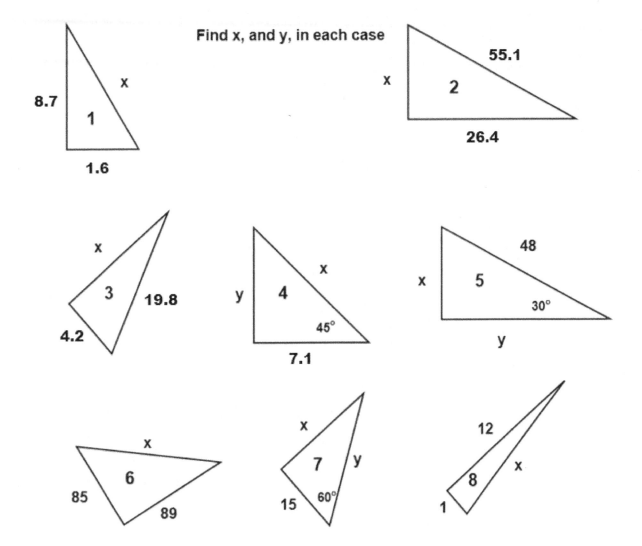

Find x, and y, in each case

RIGHT TRIANGLES

Find **x** and **y** in each of the Exercises below.

You will typically use the **Pythagorean Theorem** and a calculator.

All triangles below are **right triangles**.

Find x, and y, in each case

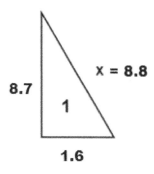

8.7
x = 8.8
1
1.6

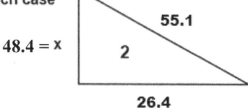

55.1
48.4 = x
2
26.4

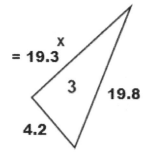

x
= 19.3
3
19.8
4.2

y
= 7.1
x 10.0
4
45°
7.1

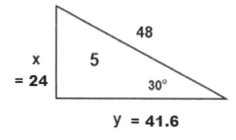

48
x
= 24
5
30°
y = 41.6

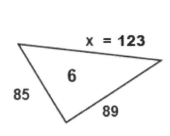

x = 123
6
85
89

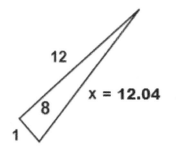

x
= 26
7
y = 30
15
60°

12
x = 12.04
8
1

RIGHT TRIANGLES

Find the unknowns, x and y.

1.

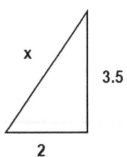

x

3.5

2

2.

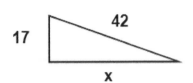

17

42

x

3.

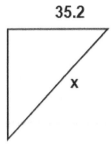

35.2

43.5

x

4

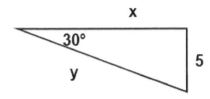

x

30°

y

5

5.

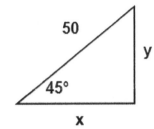

50

y

45°

x

6.

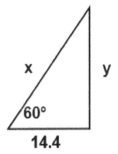

x

y

60°

14.4

RIGHT TRIANGLES

1.

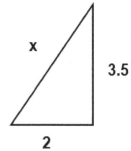

x = 4.03

2.

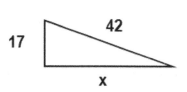

x = 38.41

3.

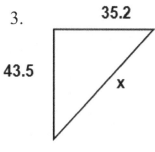

x = 55.95

4.

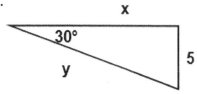

x = 8.66, y = 10

5.

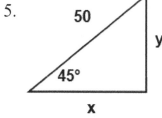

x = 35.36, y = 35.36

6.

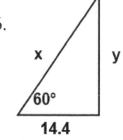

x = 28.8, y = 24.94

G6 LESSON: SIMILAR TRIANGLES

Two Triangles are similar if they have equal angles.

This means they have the same "**shape**" but may be of different sizes. If they also are the same size they are **congruent**.

Similar triangles appear frequently in practical problems.

Their corresponding ratios are equal, and that is what makes them so important and useful.

This is often the way you set up an **Equation** to find an **Unknown**.

Note: If **two** sets of angles are equal, the **third** must be equal also, and the triangles are similar.

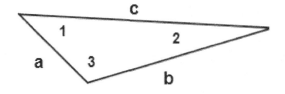 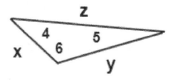

Given: 1 = 4 ; 2 = 5 ; 3 = 6, Called corresponding angles

Corresponding sides are: $a \leftrightarrow x$; $b \leftrightarrow y$; $c \leftrightarrow z$

The Following Ratios are Equal

$a/x = b/y = c/z$ and $x/a = y/b = z/c$

$a/b = x/y$ $a/c = x/z$ $b/c = y/z$

$b/a = y/x$ $c/a = z/x$ $c/b = z/y$

When you have **two equal ratios** with one **unknown** it is a simple algebra problem to solve for the unknown X.

X/a = b/c **and** X = a(b/c)   X/3 = 7/12 **and** X = 3x(7/12) = 1.75

a/X = b/c **and** X = a(c/b)   3/X = 7/12 **and** X = 3x(12/7) = 5.15

Find two similar triangles where the **unknown** is one side and you know three more sides, one of which is opposite the corresponding angle of the unknown.

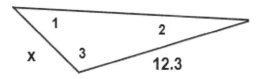

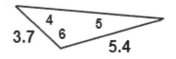

Given: 1 = 4 ; 2 = 5 ; 3 = 6   Find x

x/ 12.3 = 3.7/5.4 so x = 12.3(3.7/5.4) = 8.4

or x/3.7 = 12.3/5.4 so x = 3.7(12.3/5.4) = 8.4

Wrong: x/3.7 = 5.4/12.3   See why?

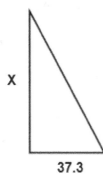

How tall is the Pole? The horizontal lines are shadows

x/5.87 = 37.3/3.42

x = 5.87(37.3.3/3.42)

= 64.02 = 64.0

SIMILAR TRIANGLES

In each Exercise assume the triangles are similar.

Find lengths that you can.

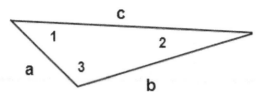 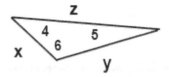

Given: <1 = <4 and <2 = <5

1. What can you conclude about <3 and <6 and why?

2. What are the corresponding sides in pairs?

3. a = 12.3, b = 18.7, x = 5.4, y = ?, z = ?

4. c = 1435, z = 765, y = 453, What can you figure?

5. a = .05, x = .02, y = .04, What can you figure?

6. c = 4, b = 3, x = 1.5, What can you figure?

7. b = 23/8, x = 3/4, y = 4/5, What can you figure?

8. In Drawing below, how tall is the pole?

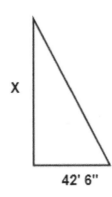

How tall is the Pole? The horizontal lines are shadows

Hint: 1" = 1/12', So, 5'8" = (58/12)'

X

42' 6"

5' 8"

3' 4"

SIMILAR TRIANGLES   Answers: []

In each Exercise assume the triangles are similar. Find lengths that you can.

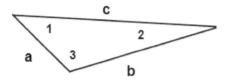 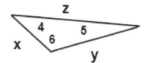

Given: <1 = <4 and <2 = <5

1. What can you conclude about <3 and <6 and why?

    [They are equal due to sum of angles of triangle equals 180°]

2. What are the corresponding sides in pairs?

    [a ↔ x, b ↔ y, c ↔ z]

3. a = 12.3, b = 18.7, x = 5.4, y = ?, z = ?

    [y = 8.2   Have not yet learned how to calculate z]

4. c = 1435, z = 765, y = 453   What can you figure?

    [b = 850]

5. a = 0.05, x = 0.02, y = 0.04   What can you figure?

    [b = 0.1]

6. c = 4, b = 3, x = 1.5   What can you figure?

    [Nothing with just similar triangles]

7. b = 2 3/8, x = 3/4 y = 4/5,   What can you figure?

    [a = 2 29/128 = 2.23]

8. In drawing below, how tall is the pole?

    [(72 1/4)' = 72' 3"]

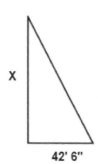

How tall is the Pole? The horizontal lines are shadows

Hint: 1" = 1/12', So, 5'8" = (58/12)'

X

5' 8"

42' 6"   3' 4"

SIMILAR TRIANGLES

Find the unknowns, x and y.

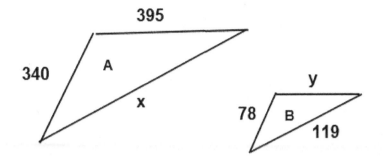

Assume that the two triangles to the left are similar. Using this knowledge, find the unknown lengths.

SIMILAR TRIANGLES

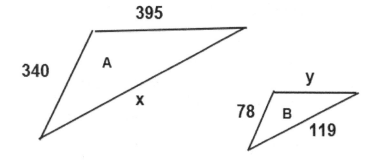

Assume that the two triangles to the left are similar. Using this knowledge, find the unknown lengths.

x = 518.72, y = 90.62

G7 LESSON: QUADRILATERALS, POLYGONS, PERIMETERS (P)

A **Polygon** is a closed geometric figure whose boundary is straight line segments. The **Perimeter** (**P**) is the distance around the polygon.

A **Quadrilateral** is a **polygon** with four sides.

Common **Quadrilaterals** are **Square**, **Rectangle**, **Rhombus**, **Parallelogram**, and **Trapezoid**.

There are three things one is usually interested in for any **quadrilateral**: **Dimensions**, **Perimeter** and **Area**.

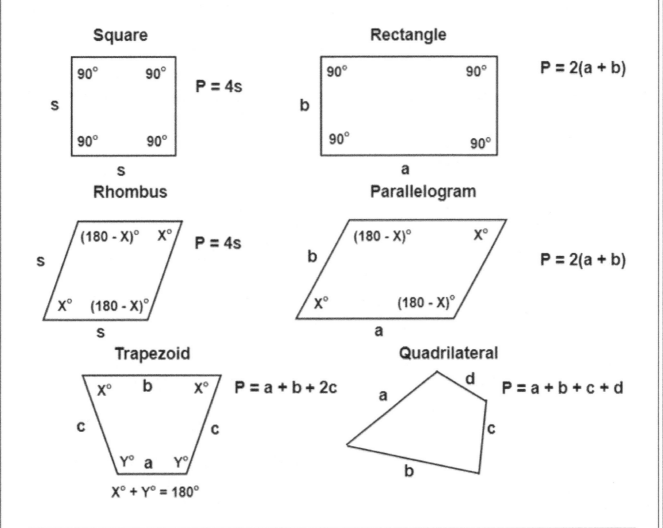

G7 Quadrilaterals, Polygons, Perimeters (P) Problems

Identify the figures below and compute their **Perimeters.**

Note: The Units of measure of the sides must be the same for all sides. For example, if one side is given in feet and the other side in inches, then you must convert one of the side's units accordingly. Must use same units for both sides.

Suppose a **rectangle** has one side 11/2 feet, and the other side 8 inches. Then, convert feet to inches or inches to feet.

Answers are at bottom of page - Number, name, Perimeter.

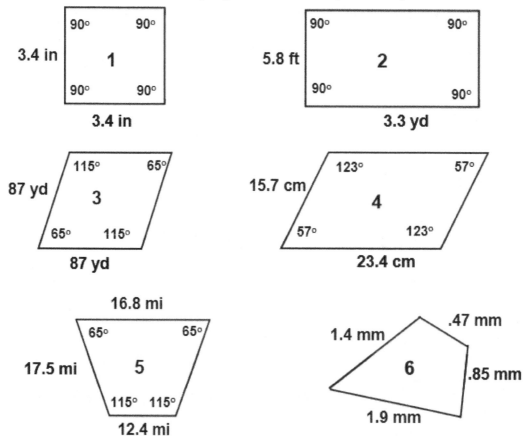

Answer: 1. Square 13.6 in   2. Rectangle 31.4 ft or 10.5 yd   3. Rhombus 348 yd

4. Parallelogram 78.2 cm   5. Trapezoid 64.2 mi   6. Quadrilateral 4.62 mm

QUADRILATERALS, POLYGONS, PERIMETERS (P)

Identify the figures below and compute their Perimeters

Note: The Units of measure of the sides must be the same for all sides. For example, if one side is given in feet and the other side in inches, then you must convert one of the side's units accordingly. Must use same units for both sides.

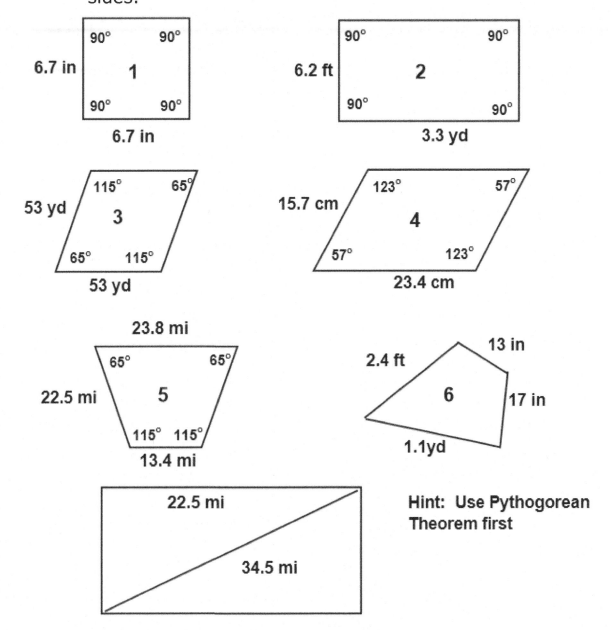

Hint: Use Pythogorean Theorem first

QUADRILATERALS, POLYGONS, PERIMETERS (P)

Identify the figures below and compute their Perimeters

Note: The Units of measure of the sides must be the same for all sides. For example, if one side is given in feet and the other side in inches, then you must convert one of the side's units accordingly. Must use same units for both sides.

Square   P = 26.8

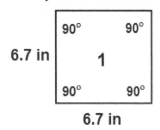

Rectangle   P = 32.2 ft = 10.7 yd

Rhombus   P = 212 yd

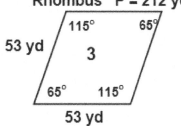

Parallelogram   P = 78.2

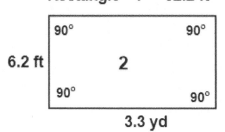

Trapezoid   P = 82.2 mi

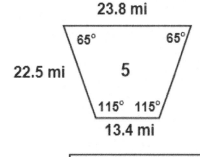

Polygon   P = 98.4 in = 8.2 ft = 2.7 yd

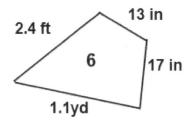

Rectangle   P = 97.3 mi

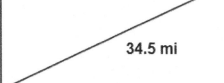

QUADRILATERALS, POLYGONS, PERIMETERS (P)

Identify the figures and calculate their perimeters. Be sure to check units and convert all numbers to the same unit where necessary.

1.

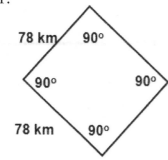

2.

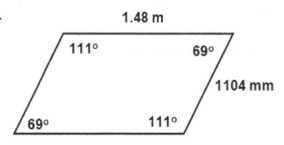

3.

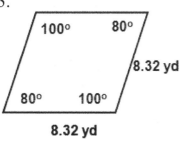

4.

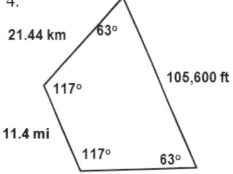

QUADRILATERALS, POLYGONS, PERIMETERS (P)

Identify the figures and calculate their perimeters. Be sure to check units and convert all numbers to the same unit where necessary.

1.

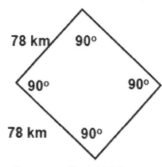

Square, P = 312 km

2.

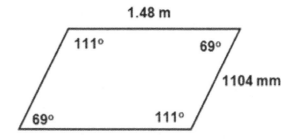

Parallelogram, P = 5.168 m = 5168mm

3.

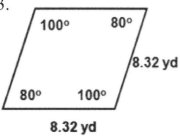

Rhombus, P = 33.28 yd

4.

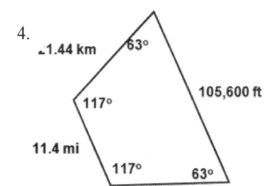

Trapezoid, P = 93.41 km = 58 mi = 306,474 ft

G8 LESSON: AREA OF TRIANGLES AND RECTANGLES

The **Area** of any **polygon** is a measure of its size.

The **Rectangle** is the simplest **polygon** and its **Area** is defined to be:

   Area = ab   where a and b are the lengths of its two sides.

A **Parallelogram** is a "**lopsided**" rectangle whose two adjacent sides have an angle $X°$ instead of $90°$.

Its **Area** can be calculated with a "**Correction Factor**" which is $SIN(X°)$

A **Triangle** is one-half of a **parallelogram**. So, its **Area** can be expressed with this same correction factor. **See Below.**

Of course, if one does know the "**height**" then one can use an alternative formula for the **Area**, which is usually given.

h = height

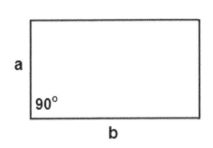

Area = ab

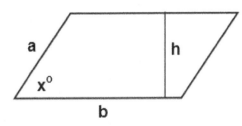

Area = abSIN(x°)
Area = hb

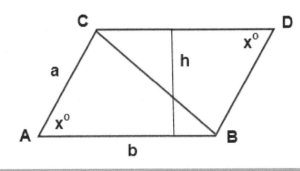

Triangle ABC = Triangle BDC

Area = .5abSIN(x°)

Area = (1/2)hb

G8 Area of Triangles and Rectangles Problems

Calculate the areas of the triangles and rectangles.

Note: The lateral units of measurement must be the same.

DO NOT multiply **ft** times **yd** for example.

Answers: # Area.

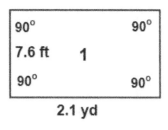

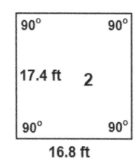

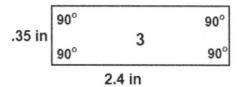

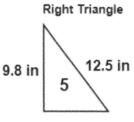

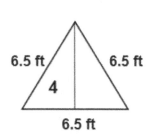

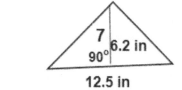

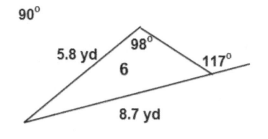

Answers: 1. 47.9 ft^2 or 5.3 yd^2 2. 292 ft^2 3. .84 in^2

4. 18.3 ft^2 5. 38 in^2 6. 8.2 yd^2 7. 38.8 in^2

AREA OF TRIANGLES AND RECTANGLES

Calculate the areas of the triangles and rectangles.

Note: The lateral units of measurement must be the same.

1.

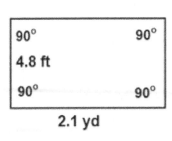

90°   90°
4.8 ft
90°   90°

2.1 yd

2.

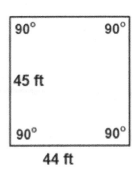

90°   90°

45 ft

90°   90°

44 ft

3.

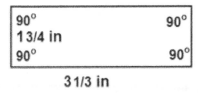

90°   90°
1 3/4 in
90°   90°

3 1/3 in

4.

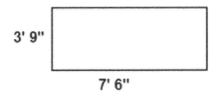

3' 9"

7' 6"

5.

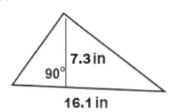

7.3 in

90°

16.1 in

6.

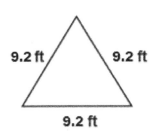

9.2 ft   9.2 ft

9.2 ft

7.

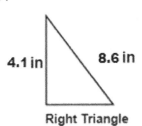

4.1 in   8.6 in

Right Triangle

8.

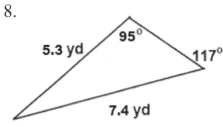

5.3 yd   95°
                        117°
7.4 yd

AREA OF TRIANGLES AND RECTANGLES

Calculate the areas of the triangles and rectangles.

Note: The lateral units of measurement must be the same.

1. **A = 30.2 ft^2 = 3.4 yd^2**

90°	90°
4.8 ft	
90°	90°

2.1 yd

2. **A = 1980 ft^2**

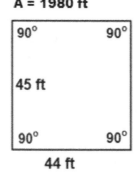

45 ft

44 ft

3. **= 5 5/6 in^2**

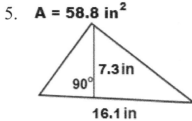

1 3/4 in

3 1/3 in

2

4.

A = 28 1/8 ft^2 = 28.125 ft^2

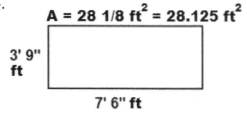

3' 9"
ft

7' 6" ft

5. **A = 58.8 in^2**

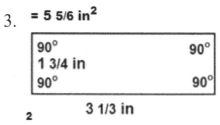

7.3 in

90°

16.1 in

6. **A = 36.7 ft^2**

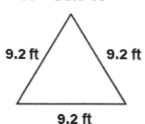

9.2 ft   9.2 ft

9.2 ft

7. **A = 15.6 in^2**

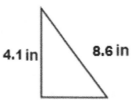

4.1 in   8.6 in

Right Triangle

8. **A = 7.35 yd^2**

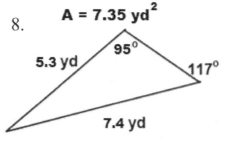

5.3 yd   95°

117°

7.4 yd

AREA OF TRIANGLES AND RECTANGLES

Identify the figures and calculate their areas. Be sure to check units and convert all numbers to the same unit where necessary.

1.

15 ft

90°   90°

15 ft

90°   90°

2.

9' 2"

90°   90°

90°   90°

4' 11"

3.

25 m   60°

60°   60°

4.

19.2 km

24 mi

30°

AREA OF TRIANGLES AND RECTANGLES

Identify the figures and calculate their areas. Be sure to check units and convert all numbers to the same unit where necessary.

1.

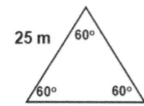

Square, A = 225 ft²

2.

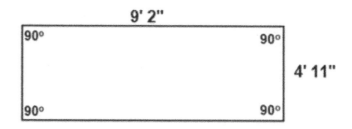

Rectangle, A = 45.07 ft²

3.

Triangle, A = 270.6 m²

4.

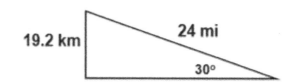

Right triangle, A = 123.7 mi² = 320.7 km²

G9 LESSON: FORMULAS FOR POLYGONS

The **Area** of any geometric object is a measure of its size.

The basic unit of **Area** measure is a **square** which measures **one linear unit (U) per side**. Then, by definition, the **Area** of such a **square is 1 U^2** of **1 Square Unit**.

The **Area** of any other closed geometric figure is defined to be the sum of **areas** of inscribed, non-overlapping, squares which are so small they fully fill up the figure.

A rigorous definition is possible, but challenging. However; intuitively, the idea of **Area** is pretty easy.

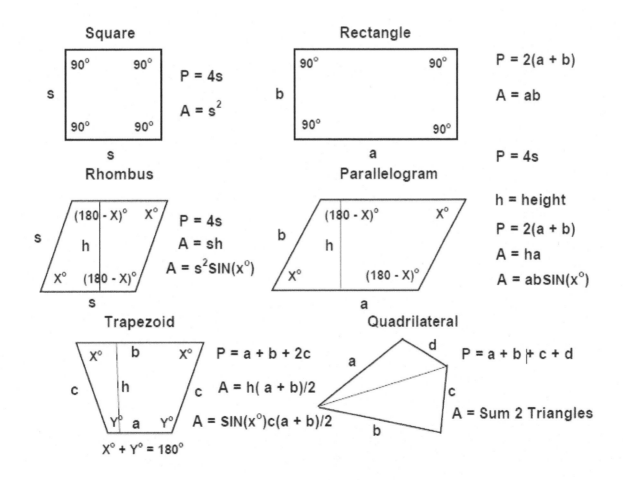

Identify the figures below and compute their Areas

Note: The Units of measure of the sides must be the same for all sides. For example, if one side is given in feet and the other side in inches, then you must convert one of the side's units accordingly. Must use same units for both sides.

Suppose a rectangle has one side 11/2 feet, and the other side 8 inches. Then, convert feet to inches.

Answers are at bottom of page # Name, Area.

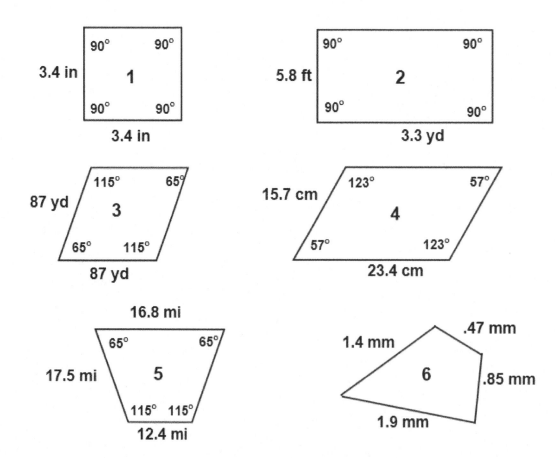

Answer: 1. Square 11.6 in^2 2. Rectangle 57.4 ft^2 or 6.4 yd^2 3. Rhombus 6860 yd^2
4. Parallelogram 308 cm^2 5. Trapezoid 231 mi^2 6. Quadrilateral Not enough Info

FORMULAS FOR POLYGONS

Identify the figures and calculate their areas.

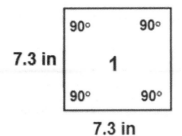

7.3 in
90° | 90°
1
90° | 90°
7.3 in

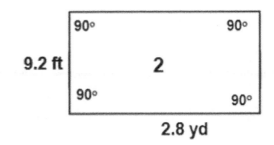

9.2 ft
90° | 90°
2
90° | 90°
2.8 yd

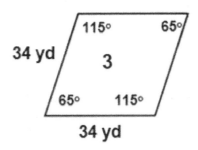

34 yd
115° | 65°
3
65° | 115°
34 yd

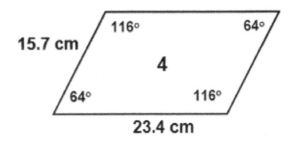

15.7 cm
116° | 64°
4
64° | 116°
23.4 cm

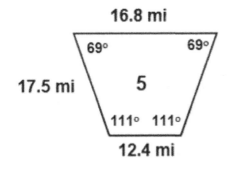

16.8 mi
69° | 69°
5
17.5 mi
111° | 111°
12.4 mi

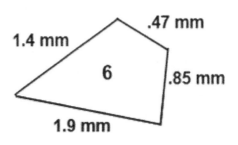

.47 mm
1.4 mm
6
.85 mm
1.9 mm

3 3/4 ft
7
5 5/8 ft

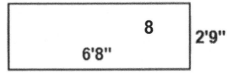

8
2'9"
6'8"

FORMULAS FOR POLYGONS

Identify the figures and calculate their areas.

Square   A = 53.3 in^2

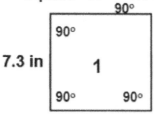

7.3 in

90° 90° 90° 90°

1

7.3 in

Rectangle   A = 8.6 yd^2 = 77.3 ft^2

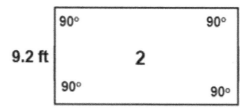

9.2 ft

90° 90° 90° 90°

2

2.8 yd

Rhombus   A = 1048 yd^2

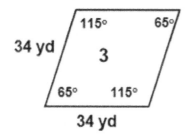

34 yd

115° 65° 65° 115°

3

34 yd

Parallelogram   A = 330.2cm^2

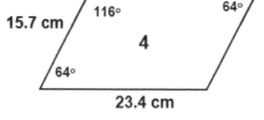

15.7 cm

116° 64° 64°

4

23.4 cm

Trapezoid   A = 238.5 mi^2

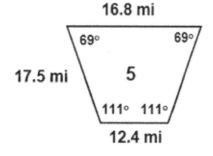

16.8 mi

69° 69°

17.5 mi

5

111° 111°

12.4 mi

Polygon   A = Insufficient Information

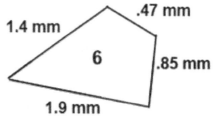

.47 mm

1.4 mm

6

.85 mm

1.9 mm

Rectangle   A = 21 3/32 ft^2 = 21.1ft^2

3 3/4 ft

7

5 5/8 ft

Rectangle   A = 18 1/3 ft^2

8

6'8"

2'9"

FORMULAS FOR POLYGONS

Identify the figures and calculate their areas.

1.

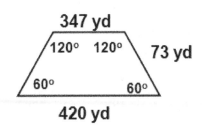

347 yd
120° 120° 73 yd
60°   60°
420 yd

2.

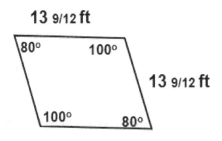

13 9/12 ft
80°   100°
13 9/12 ft
100°   80°

3.

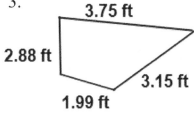

3.75 ft
2.88 ft
3.15 ft
1.99 ft

4.

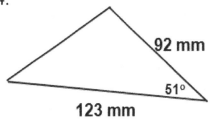

92 mm
51°
123 mm

FORMULAS FOR POLYGONS

Identify the figures and calculate their areas.

1.

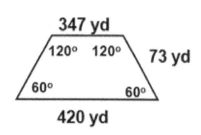

347 yd
120° 120°
73 yd
60° 60°
420 yd

Trapezoid, A = 24,244.81 yd²

2.

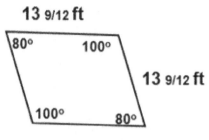

13 9/12 ft
80° 100°
13 9/12 ft
100° 80°

Rhombus, A = 186.2 ft²

3.

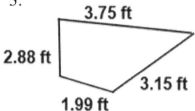

3.75 ft
2.88 ft
3.15 ft
1.99 ft

Polygon, A = Insufficient Information

4.

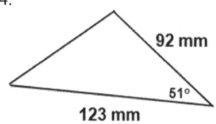

92 mm
51°
123 mm

Triangle, A = 4,397.1 mm²

A **Circle** is a set of points equidistant from a point called the Center. This distance is called the **Radius** of the circle.

The distance across the **Circle** from one side to the other through the center is called the **Diameter** = 2×**Radius**

The **Circumference**, (C) of the **Circle** is the distance around the **Circle**, sort of its **perimeter**.

The ratio of the **Circumference** to the **Diameter** is always the same number for any circle. It is called **Pi** or π

Thus $C = \pi D = 2\pi R$

π = 3.141592654 . . .   22/7 is an approximation.

I usually use 3.14 unless I need a lot of accuracy, then I use 3.1416. π is called a "**transcendental number**."

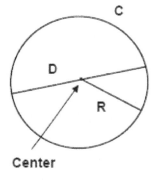
Center

R = Radius = Distance from center to any point on the circle.

D = Diameter = Distance across circle

C = Circumference

$C = \pi D = 2\pi R$

The TI 30XA has a "π **Key**" we will use for π.

The three formulas we must remember are:

$$D = 2R \quad \text{and} \quad C = 2\pi R \quad \text{and} \quad A = \pi R^2 \text{ (next lesson)}$$

Find the unknown in the following problems.

Answers: **#, R, D, C**

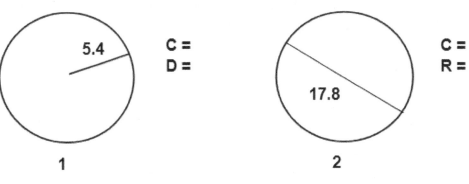

1

2

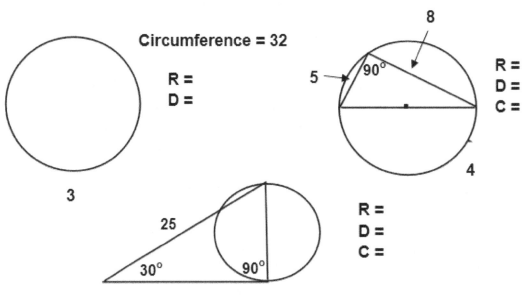

3

4

5

Answers   1. 5.4, 10.8, 33.9   2. 8.9, 17.8, 55.9   3. 5.1, 10.2, 32   4. 4.7, 9.4, 29.6
5. 6.25, 12.5, 39.3

CIRCLES π CIRCUMFERENCE

R = Radius   D = Diameter   C = Circumference

Find Unknowns

1.

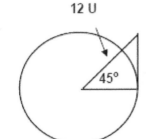

6.7 U

C = ? U
D = ? U

2.

12.3 U

C = ? U
R = ? U

3.

C = 53 U

R = ? U
D = ? U

4.

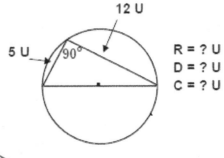

12 U

5 U   90°

R = ? U
D = ? U
C = ? U

5.

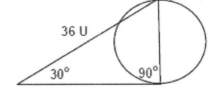

36 U

30°   90°

R = ? U
D = ? U
C = ? U

6.

12 U

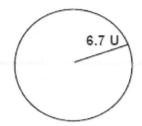

45°

R = ? U
D = ? U
C = ? U

7.

Inner Circle C = 15

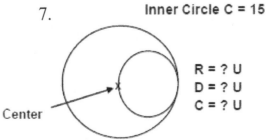

Center

R = ? U
D = ? U
C = ? U

CIRCLES π CIRCUMFERENCE

R = Radius   **D** = Diameter   **C** = Circumference

Find Unknowns

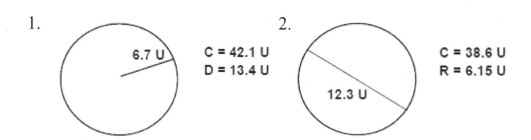

1.

6.7 U

C = 42.1 U
D = 13.4 U

2.

12.3 U

C = 38.6 U
R = 6.15 U

3.

C = 53 U

R = 8.4 U
D = 16.9 U

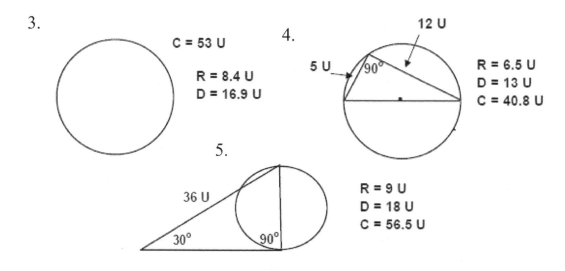

4.

12 U

5 U   90°

R = 6.5 U
D = 13 U
C = 40.8 U

5.

36 U

30°   90°

R = 9 U
D = 18 U
C = 56.5 U

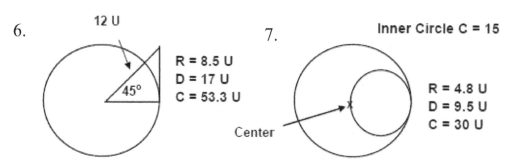

6.

12 U

45°

R = 8.5 U
D = 17 U
C = 53.3 U

7.

Inner Circle C = 15

Center

R = 4.8 U
D = 9.5 U
C = 30 U

CIRCLES π CIRCUMFERENCE

Identify the figures and calculate their perimeters. Be sure to check units and convert all numbers to the same unit where necessary.

1.

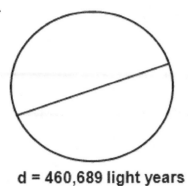

d = 460,689 light years

2.

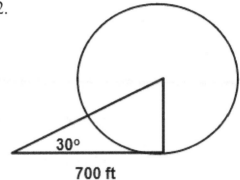

700 ft

CIRCLES π CIRCUMFERENCE

Identify the figures and calculate their perimeters. Be sure to check units and convert all numbers to the same unit where necessary.

1.

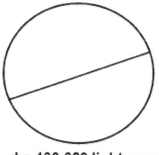

d = 460,689 light years

Circle, C = 460,689π ly = 1,447,297.2 ly

2.

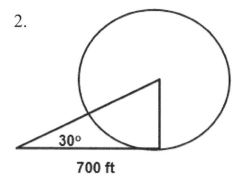

700 ft

Circle, C = 2539.32 ft

G11 LESSON: CIRCLES   AREA $A = \pi R^2$

A **Circle** is a set of points equidistant from a point called the **Center**.   This distance is called the **Radius** of the **circle**.

π is defined to be **C/D = Circumference/Diameter**

The **Area (A)** of the **Circle** turns out to be $A = \pi R^2$

This is a remarkable fact first discovered by the Greek genius mathematician **Archimedes**. It now is very easy to calculate the **Area** of any **Circle** using a calculator.

Remember: π is about 3.14

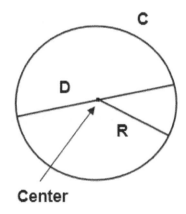

R = Radius = Distance from center to any point on the circle.

D = Diameter = Distance across circle

C = Circumference

$C = \pi D = 2\pi R$

$A = \pi R^2$

Archimedes "Proof" of Area. $A = (C/2)x(D/2) = (2\pi R/2)x(2R/2) = \pi R^2$

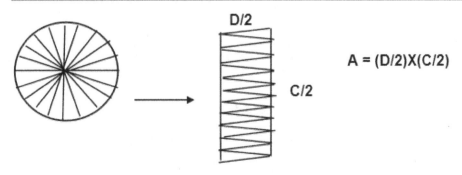

$A = (D/2)X(C/2)$

G11 Circles π Area Problems

The TI 30XA has a "_π_ **Key**" we will use for π.

The three formulas we must remember are:

$$D = 2R \quad \text{and} \quad C = 2\pi R \quad \text{and} \quad A = \pi R2 \text{ (next lesson)}$$

Find the Area in the following problems.

Answers: #, R, A

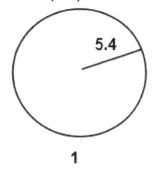

R =
A =

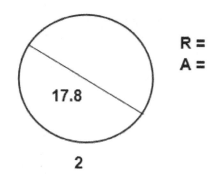

R =
A =

1

2

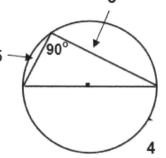

Circumference = 32

R =
A =

R =
A =

3

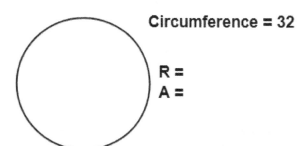

R =
A =

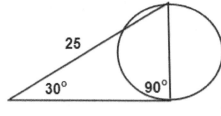

5

Answers 1. 5.4, 91.6   2. 8.9, 249   3. 5.1, 81.5   4. 4.7, 70
          5. 6.25, 123

CIRCLES π AREA

R = Radius,   **D** = Diameter,   **C** = Circumference

Find Area

1.
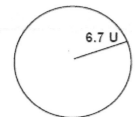
A = ? U^2

2.
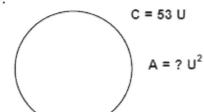
A = ? U^2

3.
C = 53 U

A = ? U^2

4.
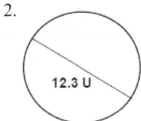
A = ? U^2

5.
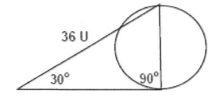
A = ? U^2

6.
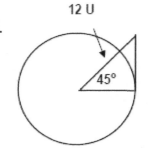
A = ? U^2

7.
Inner Circle C = 15
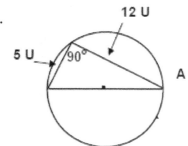
A = ? U^2

CIRCLES π AREA

R = Radius,   D = Diameter,   C = Circumference

Find Area

1.
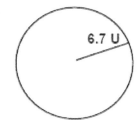
6.7 U   A = 141 U²

2.
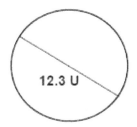
12.3 U   A = 118.8 U²

3.
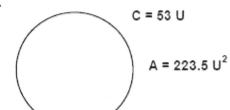
C = 53 U

A = 223.5 U²

4.
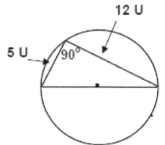
12 U
5 U   90°
A = 132.7 U²

5.
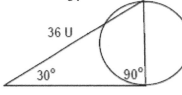
36 U
30°   90°
A = 254.5 U²

6.
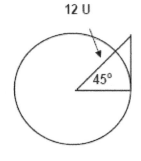
12 U
45°
A = 226.2   U²

7.
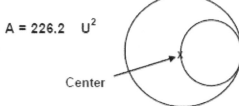
Inner Circle C = 15
A = 71.6 U²
Center

CIRCLES π AREA

Calculate the areas of the figures below. Be sure to treat units appropriately!

R = Radius,   D = Diameter,   C = Circumference

1.
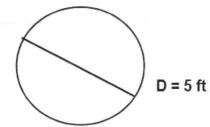
D = 5 ft

2.
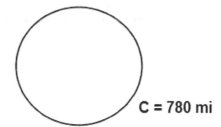
C = 780 mi

3.
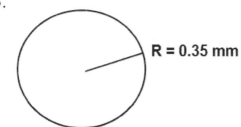
R = 0.35 mm

4.
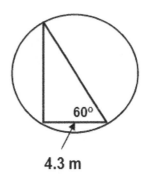
60°

4.3 m

5.
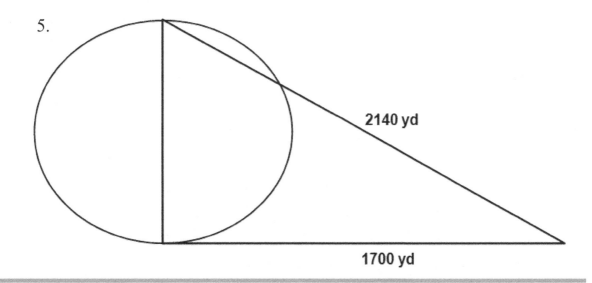
2140 yd

1700 yd

CIRCLES π AREA

Calculate the areas of the figures below. Be sure to treat units appropriately!

R = Radius,   **D** = Diameter,   **C** = Circumference

1.

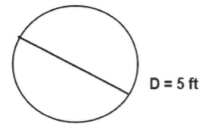

D = 5 ft

A = 19.6 ft²

2.

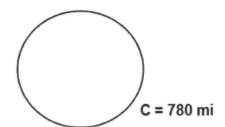

C = 780 mi

A = 48,415 mi²

3.

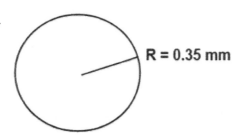

R = 0.35 mm

A = 0.385 mm²

4.

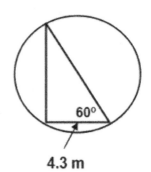

60°

4.3 m

A = 58.09 m²

5.

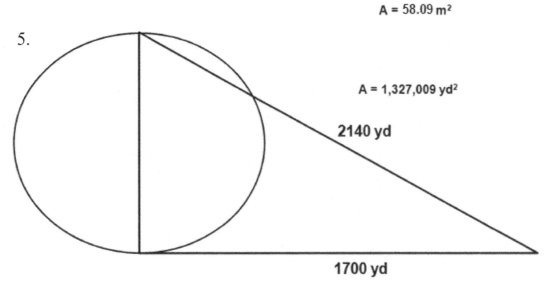

A = 1,327,009 yd²

2140 yd

1700 yd

G12 LESSON: CIRCLES   SPECIAL PROPERTIES

There are three facts about **circles** that I find useful sometimes in a practical problem.

I will present them to you with examples below:

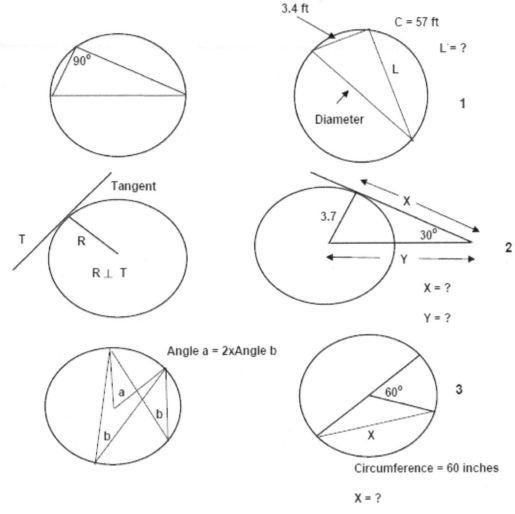

Answers: 1. 17.8   2. Y = 7.4, X = 6.4   3. X = 16.5

CIRCLES   SPECIAL PROPERTIES

There are three facts about **circles** that I find useful sometimes in a practical problem.

Find the Unknowns.

1.

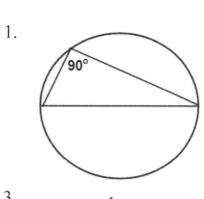

2.

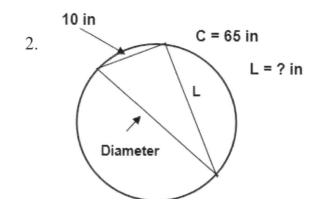

10 in

C = 65 in

L = ? in

Diameter

3.

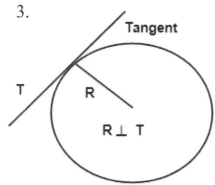

Tangent

T

R

R ⊥ T

4.

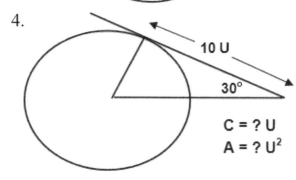

10 U

30°

C = ? U

A = ? U²

5.

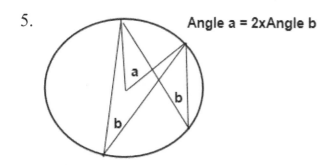

Angle a = 2xAngle b

a

b

b

6.

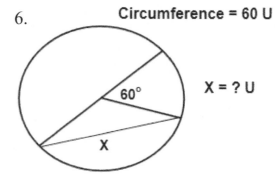

Circumference = 60 U

60°

X = ? U

X

CIRCLES   SPECIAL PROPERTIES

There are three facts about **circles** that I find useful sometimes in a practical problem.

Find the Unknowns.

1.

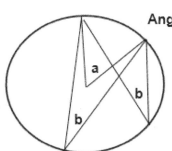

90°

2.

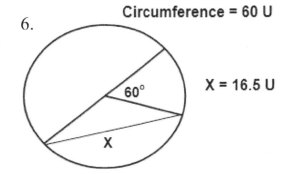

10 in

C = 65 in

L = 18.1 in

L

Diameter

3.

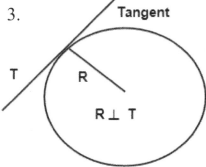

Tangent

T

R

R ⊥ T

4.

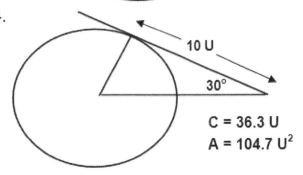

10 U

30°

C = 36.3 U

A = 104.7 U²

5.

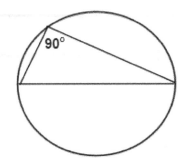

Angle a = 2xAngle b

a

b

b

6.

Circumference = 60 U

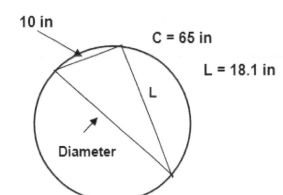

60°

X = 16.5 U

X

G13 LESSON: SURFACE AREAS   BLOCKS AND CYLINDERS

Calculate the Area of each "**face**" or "**side**" for a block.

The **Ends** and then the **Lateral Area** for the **Cylinder**

Area is measured in **Square Units, U^2**

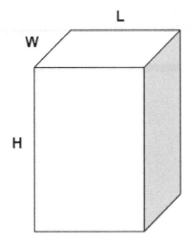

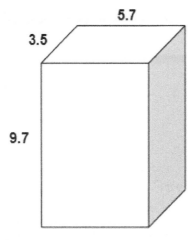

A = 2HL + 2HW + 2LW

= 2(HL + HW + LW)

$A = 2(3.5 \text{x} 5.7 + 3.5 \text{x} 9.7 + 5.7 \text{x} 9.7) = 218 \, U^2$

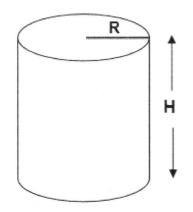

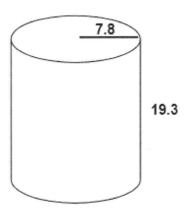

A = 2πR^2 + 2πRH

= 2πR(R + H)

$A = 2\text{x}\pi\text{x}7.8^2 + 2\pi\text{x}7.8\text{x}19.3 = 1328 \, U^2$

SURFACE AREAS BLOCKS AND CYLINDERS

Calculate the Total Surface Area, U^2, in each case.

1.

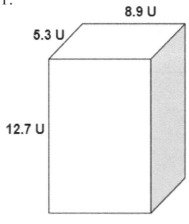

8.9 U

5.3 U

12.7 U

Area = ? U^2

2.

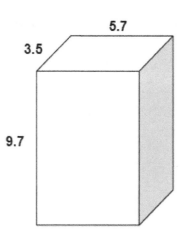

5.7

3.5

9.7

A = ? U^2

3.

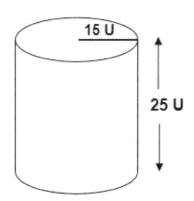

15 U

25 U

Area = ? U^2

4.

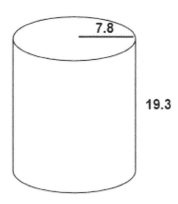

7.8

19.3

A = ? U^2

5.

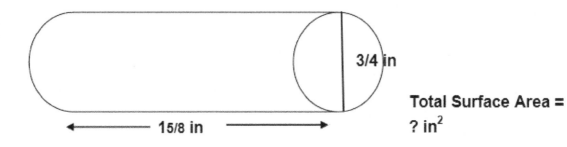

3/4 in

15/8 in

Total Surface Area = ? in^2

SURFACE AREAS BLOCKS AND CYLINDERS

Calculate the Total Surface Area, U^2, in each case.

1.

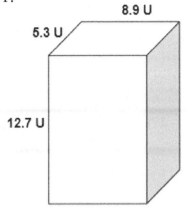

Area = 455 U^2

2.

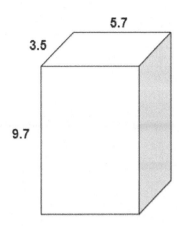

A = 2(3.5x5.7 + 3.5x9.7 + 5.7x9.7) = 218 U^2

3.

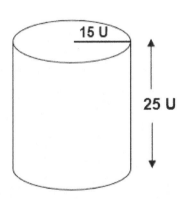

Area = 3770 U^2

4.

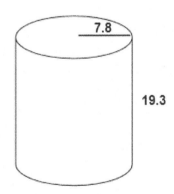

A = 2πx7.8^2 + 2πx7.8x19.3 = 1328 U^2

5.

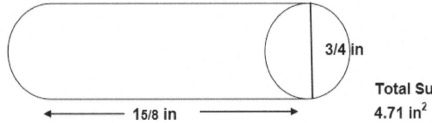

Total Surface Area = 4.71 in^2

SURFACE AREAS BLOCKS AND CYLINDERS

Calculate the surface area of the figures below. Be sure to treat units appropriately!

1.

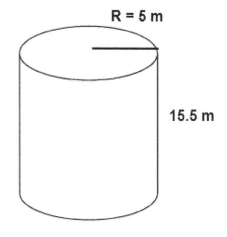

R = 5 m

15.5 m

2.

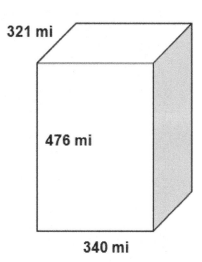

321 mi

476 mi

340 mi

3.

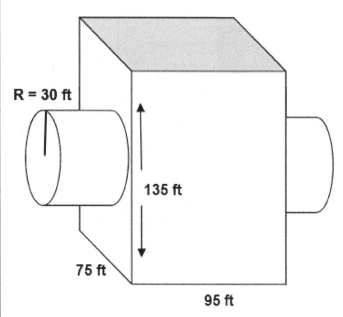

R = 30 ft

135 ft

75 ft

95 ft

Note: the cylinder of length 140 ft is centered inside the block.

4.

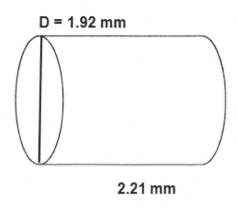

D = 1.92 mm

2.21 mm

SURFACE AREAS BLOCKS AND CYLINDERS

Calculate the surface area of the figures below. Be sure to treat units appropriately!

1.

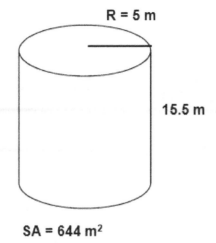

R = 5 m

15.5 m

SA = 644 m²

2.

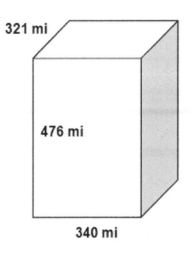

321 mi

476 mi

340 mi

SA = 847,552 mi²

3.

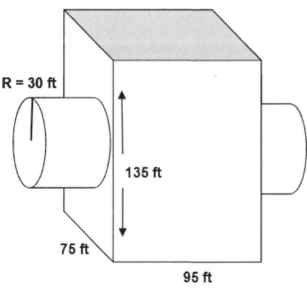

R = 30 ft

135 ft

75 ft

95 ft

Note: the cylinder of length 140 ft is centered inside the block.

SA = 68,632.3 ft²

4.

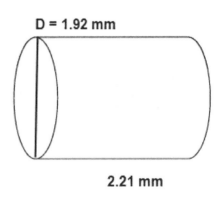

D = 1.92 mm

2.21 mm

SA = 19.12 mm²

G14 LESSON: SURFACE AREAS   CONES

If a **Cone** has **Radius, R,** for its **Base** and has **Height, H,** and **Length, L,** then its **Surface Area** consist of the area of the **Base** plus its **Lateral Area.**

Base Area = πR^2 and **Lateral Area** = $\pi R L = \pi R \sqrt{R^2 + H^2}$

Total Area = $\pi R(R + L)$ measured in U^2

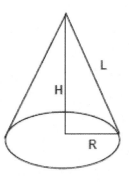

Base Area = πR^2

Lateral Area = $\pi R L$

Total Area = $\pi R(R + L)$

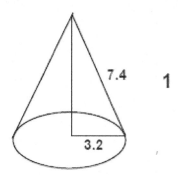

1

Find Base, Lateral, Total Areas

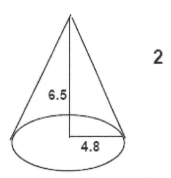

2

Find Base, Lateral, Total Areas

Answers: 1. 32.2, 74.4, 106.6 U2   2. 72.4, 121.8, 194.2 U^2

SURFACE AREAS   CONES

Find the **Base Area, BA**

Find the **Lateral Area, LA**

Find the **Total Area, TA**

1.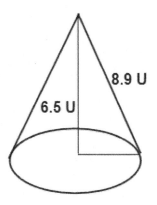

BA = ? U^2

LA = ? U^2

TA = ? U^2

2.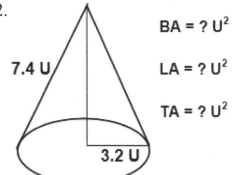

BA = ? U^2

LA = ? U^2

TA = ? U^2

3.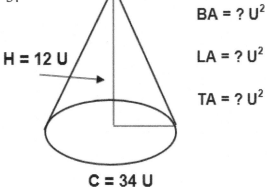

BA = ? U^2

LA = ? U^2

TA = ? U^2

4.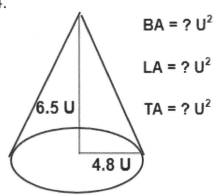

BA = ? U^2

LA = ? U^2

TA = ? U^2

SURFACE AREAS   CONES

Find the **Base Area, BA**

Find the **Lateral Area, LA**

Find the **Total Area, TA**

1.

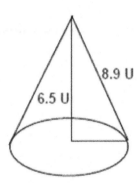

BA = 116 U²

LA = 170 U²

TA = 286 U²

8.9 U

6.5 U

2.

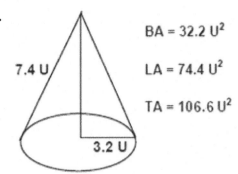

BA = 32.2 U²

LA = 74.4 U²

TA = 106.6 U²

7.4 U

3.2 U

3.

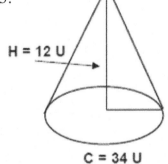

BA = 92 U²

LA = 224 U²

TA = 316 U²

H = 12 U

C = 34 U

4.

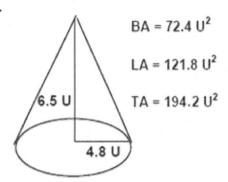

BA = 72.4 U²

LA = 121.8 U²

TA = 194.2 U²

6.5 U

4.8 U

SURFACE AREAS   CONES

Find the **Base Area, BA**

Find the **Lateral Area**, LA

Find the **Total Area, TA**

1.

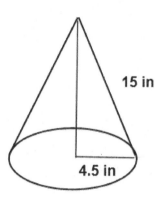

15 in

4.5 in

2.

6.5 mi

C = 8.9 mi

3.

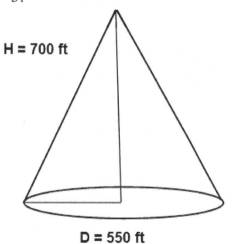

H = 700 ft

D = 550 ft

4.

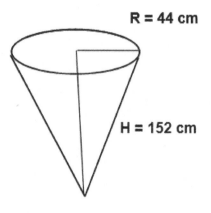

R = 44 cm

H = 152 cm

SURFACE AREAS   CONES

Find the **Base Area, BA**

Find the **Lateral Area, LA**

Find the **Total Area, TA**

1.

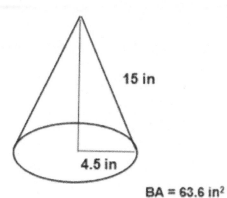

15 in

4.5 in

BA = 63.6 in²

LA= 212.1 in²

TA = 275.7 in²

2.

BA = 6.3 mi²

LA= 28.9 mi²

TA = 35.2 in²

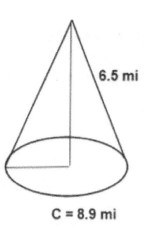

6.5 mi

C = 8.9 mi

3.

H = 700 ft

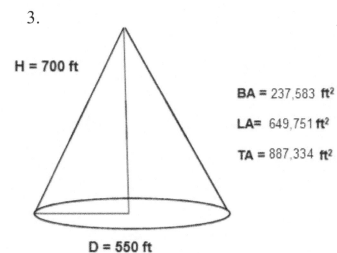

BA = 237,583 ft²

LA= 649,751 ft²

TA = 887,334 ft²

D = 550 ft

4.

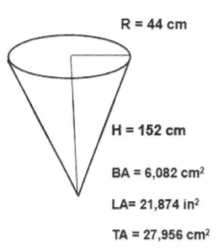

R = 44 cm

H = 152 cm

BA = 6,082 cm²

LA= 21,874 in²

TA = 27,956 cm²

G15 LESSON: VOLUMES   BLOCKS AND CYLINDERS

Volume = (Area of Base) x Height

Volume is measured in Cubic Units, U^3

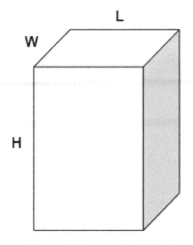

$$A = 2HL + 2HW + 2LW$$

$$V = LWH$$

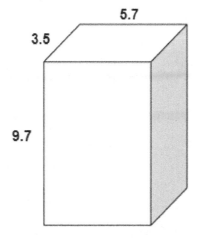

$A = 2(3.5x5.7 + 3.5x9.7 + 5.7x9.7) = 218\ U^2$

$V = 3.5x5.7x9.7 = 194\ U^3$

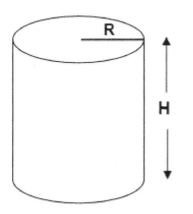

$$A = 2\pi R^2 + 2\pi RH$$

$$= 2\pi R(R + H)$$

$$V = \pi R^2 H$$

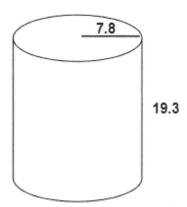

$A = 2x\pi x7.8^2 + 2\pi x7.8x19.3 = 1328\ U^2$

$V = \pi x7.8^2 x19.3 = 1174\ U^3$

VOLUMES   BLOCKS AND CYLINDERS

Calculate the **Volume, U^3**, in each case.

1.

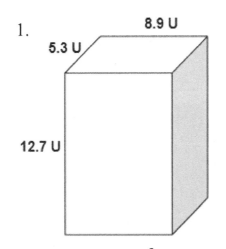

8.9 U
5.3 U
12.7 U

Volume = ? U^3

2.

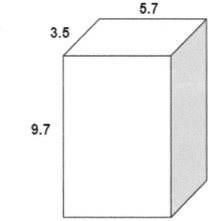

5.7
3.5
9.7

Volume = ? U^3

3.

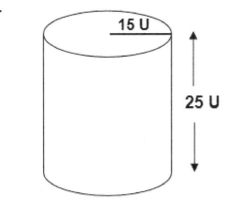

15 U
25 U

Volume = ? U^3

4.

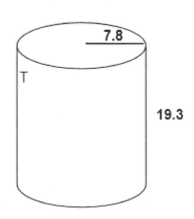

7.8
T
19.3

Volume = ? U^3

5.

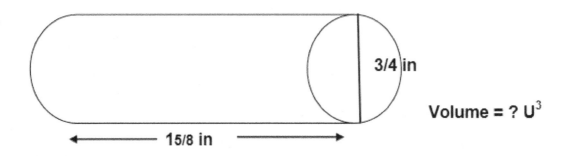

3/4 in
15/8 in

Volume = ? U^3

VOLUMES   BLOCKS AND CYLINDERS

Calculate the **Volume, U^3**, in each case.

1.

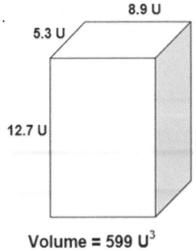

8.9 U
5.3 U
12.7 U

Volume = 599 U^3

2.

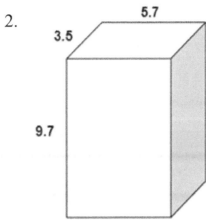

5.7
3.5
9.7

Volume = 193.5 U^3

3.

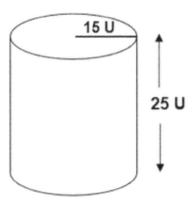

15 U
25 U

Volume = 17,671 U^3

4.

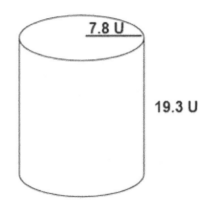

7.8 U
19.3 U

Volume = 3689 U^3

5.

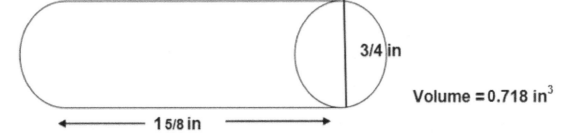

3/4 in
1 5/8 in

Volume = 0.718 in^3

VOLUMES   BLOCKS AND CYLINDERS

Find the volumes of the figures below. Be mindful of units!

1.
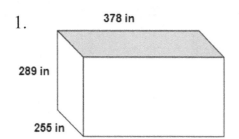
378 in

289 in

255 in

2.
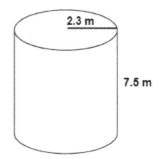
2.3 m

7.5 m

3.
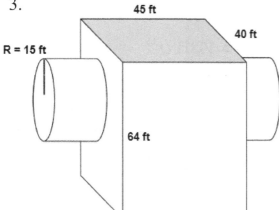
45 ft

40 ft

R = 15 ft

64 ft

The cylinder of length 65 ft is centered inside the block.

4.
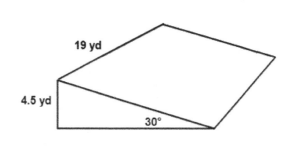
19 yd

4.5 yd

30°

VOLUMES   BLOCKS AND CYLINDERS

Find the volumes of the figures below.   Be mindful of units!

1.

378 in

289 in

255 in

V = 27,856,710 in³

2.

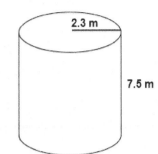

2.3 m

7.5 m

V = 124.6 m³

3.

45 ft

40 ft

R = 15 ft

64 ft

The cylinder of length 65 ft is centered inside the block.

V = 129,337 ft³

4.

19 yd

4.5 yd

30°

V = 333.2 yd³

G16 LESSON: VOLUME CONES

If a **Cone** has **Radius, R,** for its **Base** and has **Height, H,** and **Length, L,** then its **Volume, V,** is:

Base Area $= \pi R^2$ and $V = (1/3)\pi R^2 H = (1/3)\pi R^2 \sqrt{L^2 - R^2}$

Volume is measured in **Cubic Units, U^3,** where **U** is a **linear** measure.

For example: cubic inches, in^3

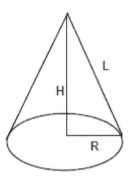

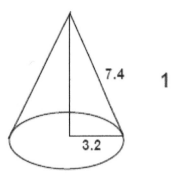

7.4   1

3.2

Find Volume

Volume $= (1/3)\pi R^2 H$

Volume $= (1/3)\pi R^2 \sqrt{L^2 - R^2}$

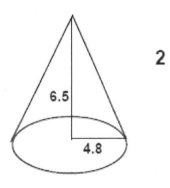

2

6.5

4.8

Find Volume

Answers: 1. 71.5 U3   2. 156.8 cubic units or U^3

VOLUMES CONES

Find the **Volume**, in U^3

1.
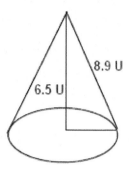
$V = ? U^3$
8.9 U
6.5 U

2.
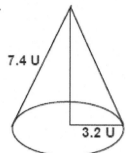
$V = ? U^3$
7.4 U
3.2 U

3.
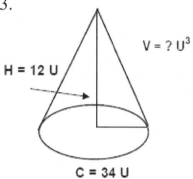
H = 12 U
$V = ? U^3$
C = 34 U

4.
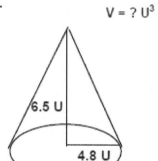
$V = ? U^3$
6.5 U
4.8 U

5.
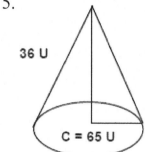
$V = ? U^3$
36 U
C = 65 U

6.
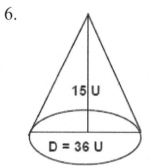
$V = ? U^3$
15 U
D = 36 U

VOLUMES CONES

Find the **Volume**, in U^3

1.

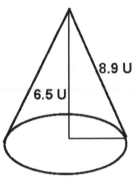

V = 251.6 U^3

8.9 U

6.5 U

2.

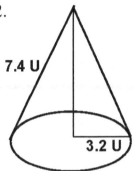

V = 71.5 U^3

7.4 U

3.2 U

3.

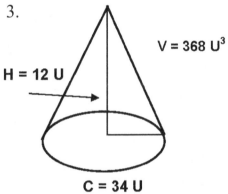

V = 368 U^3

H = 12 U

C = 34 U

4.

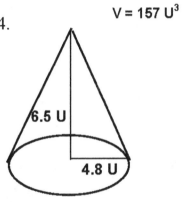

V = 157 U^3

6.5 U

4.8 U

5.

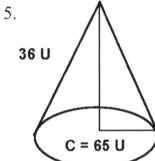

V = 3864 U^3

36 U

C = 65 U

6.

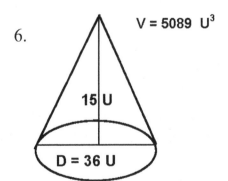

V = 5089 U^3

15 U

D = 36 U

VOLUMES CONES

Find the volume.

1.

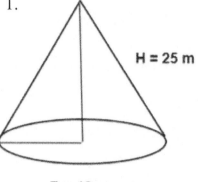

H = 25 m

R = 10 m

2.

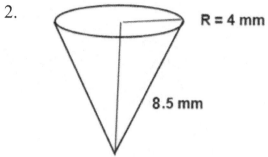

R = 4 mm

8.5 mm

3.

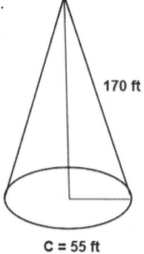

170 ft

C = 55 ft

4.

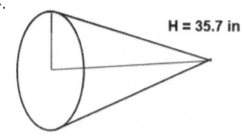

H = 35.7 in

Disk area = 25 in²

VOLUMES CONES

Find the volume.

1.

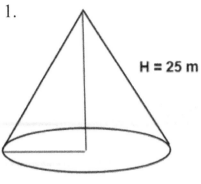

H = 25 m

R = 10 m

V = 2618 m³

2.

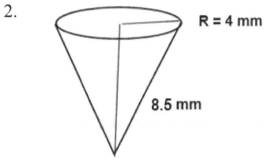

R = 4 mm

8.5 mm

V = 125.7 mm³

3.

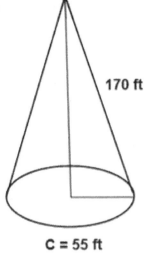

170 ft

C = 55 ft

V = 13,623 ft³

4.

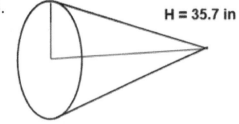

H = 35.7 in

Disk area = 25 in²

V = 297.5 in³

The **Surface Area** of a **Sphere** with **Radius, R,** in **Linear Units, U,** is:

$$A = 4\pi R^2 \text{ Square Units, } U^2$$

This is very difficult to prove and we will defer that proof until Tier 4. However, I remember it as follows:

The **Area** of the **circle** of the **cross section** of the **Sphere** through its center is πR^2. I imagine it is rubber and we blow it up like a domed tent. Then its **Area** doubles and that is a **hemisphere** of **Surface Area** $2\pi R^2$. So, the whole **Sphere** is double this, or $4\pi R^2$ U^2.

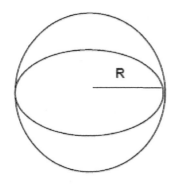

$$A = 4\pi R^2$$

Problems

R = 5.2 ft	A =	1
R = 150 mi	A =	2
R = .035 cm	A =	3
R = 1 3/4 ft	A =	4

If the **Surface Area** of a **Ball** is to be 36 sq. in., what should its **Radius** be?

$4\pi R^2 = 36$ in^2, then R = $\sqrt{36/4\pi}$ = 1.7 inches

Answers: 1. 340 ft2   2. 282,750 mi^2 3. .0154 cm^2 4. 38.5 ft^2

SURFACE AREA   BALL OR SPHERE

Find the **Surface Area** of the **Spheres** or **Balls**.

What is the formula for the **Surface Area** of a **Sphere** with **Radius R?**

How do you remember it?

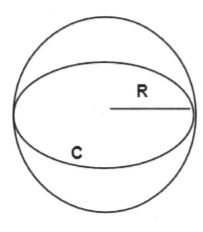

R = Radius
D = Diameter
C = Circumference

Exercises

R = 5.2 ft   A = ?

R = 150 mi   A = ?

R = .035 cm   A = ?

R = 1 3/4 ft   A = ?

C = 36 ft   A = ?

C = 120 mi   A = ?

C = 45/8 in   A = ?

D = .025 cm   A = ?

D = 68 in   A = ?

If the Surface Area of a Ball is to be 36 sq. in., what should its Radius be?

SURFACE AREA   BALL OR SPHERE   Answers: []

Find the **Surface Area** of the **Spheres** or **Balls**.

What is the formula for the Surface Area of a Sphere with
Radius R? $[4\pi R^2]$

What's one way you can remember it? [**The Cross Section of the
Ball is a circle of Radius
R and Area πR^2.**]

Now, imagine blowing this up like it's rubber until each point is R
from the center.   [**Turns out the surface area is exactly
...thus, Hemisphere area is $2\pi R^2$**]

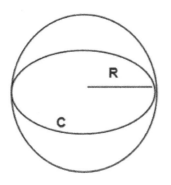

R = Radius
D = Diameter
C = Circumference

Exercises

R = 5.2 ft	A = 340 ft²
R = 150 mi	A = 282,743 mi²
R = .035 cm	A = .015 cm²
R = 1 3/4 ft	A = 38.5 ft²
C = 36 ft	A = 412.5 ft²
C = 120 mi	A = 4,584 mi²
C = 45/8 in	A = 6.8 in²
D = .025 cm	A = .002 cm²
D = 68 in	A = 14,527 in²

If the Surface Area of a Ball is to be 36 sq. in., what should its Radius be?   1.7 in

SURFACE AREA   BALL OR SPHERE

Find the surface area for the spheres with the dimensions below.

1.) Recall the formula for surface area for a sphere, SA = 4πR². If the radious doubled, how much would the SA change? What about if the radius was halved?

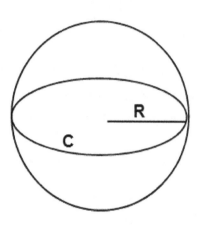

2.) R = 35 cm

3.) R = 389 mi

4.) D = 12.6 mm

5.) C = 200,209 km

6.) C = 4π ft

SURFACE AREA   BALL OR SPHERE

Find the surface area for the spheres with the dimensions below.

1.) Recall the formula for surface area for a sphere, $SA = 4\pi R^2$. If the radious doubled, how much would the SA change? What about if the radius was halved?

Answer: Because the radius is squared, doubling it would cause a 4x increase in surface area. Conversely, halving the radius would result in 4x less surface area.

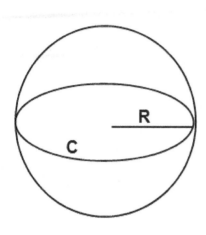

2.) R = 35 cm

SA = 15,394 cm^2

3.) R = 389 mi

SA = 1,901,556 mi^2

4.) D = 12.6 mm

SA = 498.8 mm^2

5.) C = 200,209 km

SA = 12,759,020,060 km^2

6.) C = 4π ft

SA = 50.3 ft^2

The **Volume** of a **Sphere** with **Radius, R,** in **linear units U,** is:

$$V = (4/3)\,\pi R^3 \text{ Cubic Units, } U^3$$

This is very difficult to prove and we will defer that proof until Tier 4. However, I remember it as follows:

> **Archimedes Tombstone:** Imagine a **Sphere** inscribed inside a **Cylinder.** The **Ratio** of the **Volume** or the **Sphere** to the **Volume** of the **Cylinder** is 2:3
>
> The **Cylinder** will have **Base Radius R** and **Height 2R.**
> Thus, its **Volume** will be $\pi R^2 \times 2R = 2\pi R^3$
> The **Volume** of the **Sphere** is thus, $(2/3) \times 2\pi R^3 = (4/3)\,\pi R^3$

Note: I say "**triangle**" three times instead of "**tombstone.**"

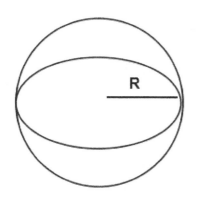

$$A = 4\pi R^2$$

$$V = (4/3)\pi R^3$$

Problems

R = 5.2 ft	V =	1
R = 150 mi	V =	2
R = .035 cm	V =	3
R = 1 3/4 ft	V =	4

If the Volume of a Ball is to be 36 cu. in., what should its Radius be?

_____

$(4/3)\pi R3 = 36$ in3, then R = $\sqrt[3]{36 \times 3/4\pi}$ = 2.05 inches

Answers 1. 589 ft^3 2. 14,137,000 mi^3 3. .00018 cm^3 4. 22.4 ft^3

VOLUME   BALL OR SPHERE

Find the **Volume** of the **Spheres** or **Balls**.

What is the formula for the **Volume** of a **Sphere** with **Radius R**?

What's one way you can remember it?

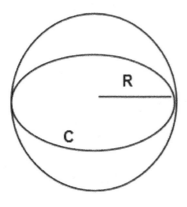

R = Radius
D = Diameter
C = Circumference

Exercises

R = 5.2 ft   V = ?

R = 150 mi   V = ?

R = .035 cm V = ?

R = 1 3/4 ft   V = ?

C = 36 ft   V = ?

C = 120 mi   V = ?

C = 45/8 in   V = ?

D = .025 cm V = ?

D = 68 in   V = ?

If the Volume of a Ball is to be 100 cu. in., what should its Radius be?

VOLUME   BALL OR SPHERE   Answers: []

Find the **Volume** of the **Spheres** or **Balls**.

What is the formula for the **Volume** of a **Sphere** with **Radius R**?

$$[(4/3) \, \pi R^3]$$

What's one way you can remember it?

[Archimedes Tombstone formula whereby the Volume of the Sphere is 2/3 the Volume of a Cylinder the Sphere is inscribed in $(2/3) \times \pi R^2 \times 2R = (4/3) \, \pi R^3$]

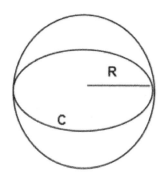

R = Radius
D = Diameter
C = Circumference

Exercises

R = 5.2 ft   V = 589 ft³

R = 150 mi   V = 14,137,167 mi³

R = .035 cm   V = .00018 cm³

R = 1 3/4 ft   V = 22.4 ft³

C = 36 ft   V = 788 ft³

C = 120 mi   V = 29,181 mi³

C = 45/8 in   V = 1.67 in³

D = .025 cm   V = .0000082 cm³

D = 68 in   V = 164,636 in³

If the Volume of a Ball is to be 100 cu. in., what should its Radius be?   2.88 in

VOLUME   BALL OR SPHERE

1.) Recall the formula for volume of a sphere, $V = (4/3)\pi R^3$. If the radius doubled, how much would the V change? What about if the radius was halved?

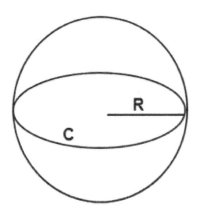

2.) R = 17 in

3.) R = 2.5 mm

4.) D = 600 mi

5.) C = 40 km

6.) C = 2π ∪

VOLUME   BALL OR SPHERE

1.) Recall the formula for volume of a sphere, $V = (4/3)\pi R^3$. If the radius doubled, how much would the V change? What about if the radius was halved?

Answer: Because the radius is cubed, increasing it by a factor of 2 would increase the volume by a factor of 8. Conversely, halving the radius would reduce the volume by a factor of 8.

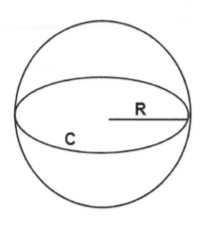

2.) R = 17 in

$V = 20,579.5 \text{ in}^3$

3.) R = 2.5 mm

$V = 65.4 \text{ mm}^3$

4.) D = 600 mi

$V = 113,097,336 \text{ mi}^3$

5.) C = 40 km

$V = 1,080.8 \text{ km}^3$

6.) C = 2π U

$V = (4/3)\pi \ U^3 = 4.19 \ U^3$

G19 LESSON: WHEN GEOMETRY IS NOT ENOUGH FOR TRIANGLES

We have learned to solve many practical problems using a combination of geometry and algebra. **Triangles** are the most common geometric figure we use in our models.

Yet, there are many practical problems involving **triangles** we still cannot solve with our current knowledge. This Lesson will point out some of these.

That's the "bad news." The "good news" is that we will be able to solve all of these problems using the tools we will learn in the last Section of the Foundation, Trigonometry.

NOTE: See if you can catch the three times I use the word triangle instead of tombstone.

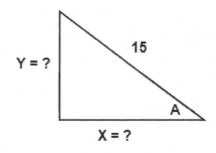

Problem: Find X and Y

If A = 30° or 45° or 60° we can solve this

With the tool of Trig, we can solve for any angle A.

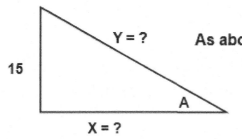

As above, we can solve for A = 30° or 45° or 60°

Trig will solve for all other angle A's

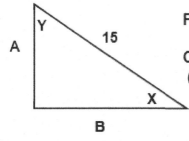

Find Angles X and Y given values of A or B.

Can Solve if A or B equals 15 times (1/2) or ($\sqrt{2.2}$) of ($\sqrt{3}/2$), not otherwise, so far.

Trig solves for any A or B

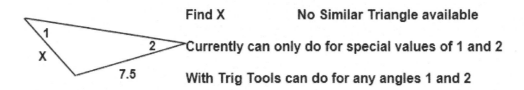

Find X   No Similar Triangle available

Currently can only do for special values of 1 and 2

With Trig Tools can do for any angles 1 and 2

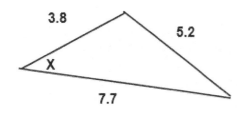

Can find X IF we have a similar triangle
with known corresponding sides

With Trig Tools Do Not need the similar triangle

Law of Sines

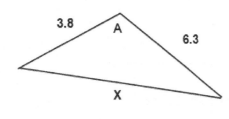

Find X

If A = 90°, OK with Pythagorean Theorem

Trig Tool for any angle A.

Generalized Pythagorean Theorem

Law of Cosines

Find Angle X

Same Trig Tool as above

Useful in finding area of this triangle

Find the Area of this Triangle

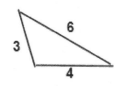

Trigonometry has many profound applications beyond practical math.

WHEN GEOMETRY IS NOT ENOUGH FOR TRIANGLES

Give four examples of **triangle** "problems" we cannot yet solve with just the geometry and algebra we have learned, but which we will be able to solve with Trig.

This is an Optional Exercise.

It is designed to help you appreciate the value the powerful Tool of Trigonometry will be for practical problem solving.

Before the scientific calculator was invented, Trig was pretty difficult to learn and apply to practical math.

Now, it is breeze. Aren't Power Tools wonderful?

HINT: Just imagine you know three of the variables below. Then can you find the others? With what you know now?
   In many cases the answer will be NO. But, with Trig you will be able to solve any solvable triangle problem!

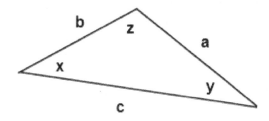

WHEN GEOMETRY IS NOT ENOUGH FOR TRIANGLES

Give four examples of **triangle** "problems" we cannot yet solve with just geometry and algebra we have learned; but, which we will be able to solve with Trig.

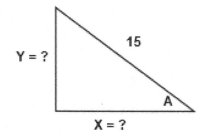

Problem: Find X and Y

If A = 30° or 45° or 60° we can solve this now

With the tool of Trig, we can solve for any angle A.

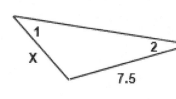

Find Angles X and Y given values of A or B.

Can Solve if A or B equals15 times
(1/2) or (√2.2) of (√3/2), not otherwise, so far.

Trig solves for any A or B

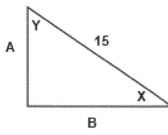

Find X   No Similar Triangle available

Currently can only do for special values of 1 and 2

With Trig Tools can do for any angles 1 and 2
    Law of Sines

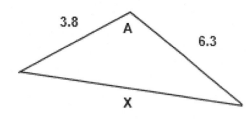

Find X or A given the other.

If A = 90°, OK with Pythagorean Theorem

Trig Tool for any angle A.

Generalized Pythogorean Theorem
Law of Cosines

INTRODUCTION TO TRIGONOMETRY

Trigonometry, **Trig,** is the study of triangles.

Trig consists of several powerful tools which will empower you to solve virtually any solvable problem with triangles including the ones discussed in Lesson G19.

It begins with the basic Trig Functions, **SIN, COS,** and **TAN**.

These are the "**power tools**" that let us solve problems.

In the old days, there were extensive Trig Tables that were used. It was arduous to learn and apply these tables.

Today, with the power tool of the TI 30XA, we can solve virtually any triangle problem in a matter of minutes or less.

Actually, in some ways Trig is easier than geometry.

We will learn how to use the three Trig Functions, and also, we will learn two very powerful theorems which make these tools even more valuable:

The **Law of Sines** (Lesson T6)

The Generalized **Pythagorean Theorem** commonly called: **The Law of Cosines** (Lesson T7)

Trigonometry then has many extensions into analytical geometry, complex numbers, calculus, and functional analysis which have profound effects in science, engineering and technology.

T1 LESSON: TRIG FUNCTIONS   SIN   COS   TAN

In any **Right Triangle**, there are **Six Ratios** of side lengths. They come in sets of three where one set is just the reciprocal of the other set.

See the triangle below: a/c, b/c, and a/b are one set.

c is called the **Hypotenuse**, or **Hyp**.

b is called the **Adjacent side** (to angle 1), or **Adj**

a is called the **Opposite side** (to angle 1, or **Opp**

So, the Ratios are   **Opp/Hyp, Adj/Hyp, Opp/Adj**

These three ratios are the three **Trig functions of angle 1**.

SIN(1) = Opp/Hyp
COS(1) = Adj/Hyp
TAN = Opp/Adj = **SIN**(1)/**COS**(1)

Angle 1 will always be measured in **degrees** $^\circ$ in this Foundation Course.

In advanced applications of Trig, angle 1 is measured in Radians, RAD.

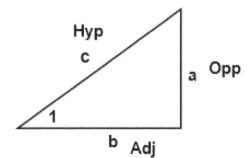

SIN (1) = a/c = Opp/Hyp

COS (1) = b/c = Adj/Hyp

TAN (1) = a/b = Opp/Adj

When turn on the TI 30XA, **DEG** always comes up.

SIN^{-1} COS^{-1} TAN^{-1}

Enter any number between -1 and 1, and find the angle whose **SIN** it is.

Ditto for **COS** and **TAN**. In other words, if

SIN (1) = a, then (1) = **SIN**$^{-1}$(a)

WARNING: See **T5** for some special information about **SIN**$^{-1}$

T1 Trig Functions SIN COS TAN Problems

Find SIN(1), COS(1), TAN (1) given angle (1) in degrees $^\circ$
Find Angle (1), Given SIN(1), COS(1) using SIN^{-1} and COS^{-1}

Problems: in $^\circ$	Angle 1	SIN(1)	COS(1)	TAN(1)
30°	0.5	0.866	0.577	
45°	0.707	0.707	1	
60°	0.866	0.5	1.732	
17°	0.292	0.956	0.306	
38°	0.616	0.788	0.781	
52.7°	0.795	0.606	1.313	
68°	0.927	0.375	2.48	
85°	0.996	0.087	11	
90°	1	0	Error	
100°	0.985	-0.174	-5.68	
115°	0.906	-0.423	-2.15	
135°	0.707	-0.707	-1	
145°	0.574	-0.819	-0.7	
150°	0.5	-0.866	-0.577	
176°	0.07	-0.998	-0.07	

Problems: Find angle 1 if

Angle (1)

	Angle (1)	
SIN(1) = 0.7865	51.9°	Note: SIN^{-1}(SIN(120°) = 60°
SIN(1) = 0.5	30°	
SIN(1) = -0.654	-40.8°	COS^{-1}(COS(120°) = 120°
COS(1) = 0.7865	38.1°	
COS(1) = 0.5	60°	
COS(1) = -0.654	130.8°	
TAN(1) = 0.7865	38.2°	
TAN(1) = 0.5	26.6°	
TAN(1) = -0.654	-33.2°	

Note: These problems are repeated on the T1E page as well.

TRIG FUNCTIONS   SIN   COS   TAN

Find $SIN(1)$, $COS(1)$, $TAN(1)$ given **angle** (1) in degrees ^{o}
Find **Angle** (1), Given $SIN(1)$, $COS(1)$ using SIN^{-1} and COS^{-1}

Angle 1	SIN(1)	COS(1)	TAN(1)	Evaluate
30°				$SIN^{-1}[COS(30^o)] = ?$
45°				$COS^{-1}[COS(30^o)] = ?$
60°				$SIN^{-1}[COS(120^o)] = ?$
17°				$COS^{-1}[SIN(120^o)] = ?$
38°				$COS^{-1}[SIN(60^o)] = ?$
52.7^o				$COS^{-1}[SIN(45^o)] = ?$
68°				$TAN^{-1}[SIN(90^o)] = ?$
85°				$SIN[COS^{-1}(0.5)] = ?$
90°				$SIN[COS^{-1}(0.867)] = ?$
100°				$COS[SIN^{-1}(0.867)] = ?$
115°				$SIN[COS^{-1}(1)] = ?$
135°				$SIN[COS^{-1}(0)] = ?$
145°				$SIN[COS^{-1}(0.707)] = ?$
150°				$TAN[SIN^{-1}(0.707)] = ?$
176°				$TAN[COS^{-1}(0.707)] = ?$

Find **angle** (1) if   Angle (1)
$SIN(1) = 0.7865$
$SIN(1) = 0.5$
$SIN(1) = -0.654$
$COS(1) = 0.7865$
$COS(1) = 0.5$
$COS(1) = -0.654$
$TAN(1) = 0.7865$
$TAN(1) = 0.5$
$TAN(1) = -0.654$

TRIG FUNCTIONS   SIN   COS   TAN

Find $SIN(1)$, $COS(1)$, $TAN(1)$ given angle (1) in **degrees** $^{\circ}$
Find **Angle** (1), Given $SIN(1)$, $COS(1)$ using SIN^{-1} and COS^{-1}

Angle 1	SIN(1)	COS(1)	TAN(1)	Evaluate	
30°	0.5	0.866	0.577	$SIN^{-1}[COS(30°)] = ?$	60°
45°	0.707	0.707	1	$COS^{-1}[COS(30°)] = ?$	30°
60°	0.866	0.5	1.732	$SIN^{-1}[COS(120°)] = ?$	-30°
17°	0.292	0.956	0.306	$COS^{-1}[SIN(120°)] = ?$	30°
38°	0.616	0.788	0.781	$COS^{-1}[SIN(60°)] = ?$	30°
52.7°	0.795	0.606	1.313	$COS^{-1}[SIN(45°)] = ?$	45°
68°	0.927	0.375	2.475	$TAN^{-1}[SIN(90°)] = ?$	45°
85°	0.996	0.087	11.43	$SIN[COS^{-1}(0.5)] = ?$	0.867
90°	1	0	Error	$SIN[COS^{-1}(0.867)] = ?$	0.5
100°	0.985	-0.174	-5.68	$COS[SIN^{-1}(0.867)] = ?$	0.5
115°	0.906	-0.423	-2.15	$SIN[COS^{-1}(1)] = ?$	0
135°	0.707	-0.707	-1	$SIN[COS^{-1}(0)] = ?$	1
145°	0.574	-0.819	-0.7	$SIN[COS^{-1}(0.707)] = ?$	0.707
150°	0.5	-0.866	-0.577	$TAN[SIN^{-1}(0.707)] = ?$	1
176°	0.07	-0.998	-0.07	$TAN[COS^{-1}(0.707)] = ?$	1

Find angle (1) if	Angle (1)
$SIN(1) = 0.7865$	51.9°
$SIN(1) = 0.5$	30°
$SIN(1) = -0.654$	-40.8°
$COS(1) = 0.7865$	38.1°
$COS(1) = 0.5$	60°
$COS(1) = -0.654$	130.8°
$TAN(1) = 0.7865$	38.2°
$TAN(1) = 0.5$	26.6°
$TAN(1) = -0.654$	-33.2

TRIG FUNCTIONS   SIN   COS   TAN

1. $x = 30°$ Find sin(x) , cos(x), and tan(x)

2. $x = 60°$ Find sin(x), cos(x), and tan(x)

3. Find $\cos^{-1}(\sin(60°)) = ?$

4. If cos(x) = 0.5   Find angle x

5. $x = 45°$ Find sin(x) cos(x) and tan(x)

6. $x = 15°$ Find sin(x), cos(x), and tan(x)

7. Find $\sin^{-1}(\cos(30°)) = ?$

8. If sin(x) = 0.315   Find angle x

9. $x = 90°$ Find sin(x), cos(x), and tan(x)

10. $x = 150°$ Find sin(x), cos(x), and tan(x)

11. Find $\sin(\cos^{-1}(0.5)) = ?$

12. If tan(x) = 0.425   Find angle x

13. $x = 117°$ Find sin(x), cos(x), and tan(x)

14. $x = 34.5°$ Find sin(x), cos(x), and tan(x)

15. Find $\sin^{-1}(\tan(17°)) = ?$

16. If sin(x) = -0.5   Find angle x

17. $x = 100°$ Find sin(x), cos(x), and tan(x)

18. $x = 0°$ Find sin(x), cos(x), and tan(x)

19. Find $\tan^{-1}(\cos(70°)) = ?$

20. If tan(x) = -0.245   Find angle x

TRIG FUNCTIONS   SIN   COS   TAN   Answers: [ ]

1. x = 30°   Find sin(x) , cos(x), and tan(x)

   [sin(30°) = 0.5, cos(30°) = 0.866, tan(30°) = 0.577]

2. x = 60° Find sin(x), cos(x), and tan(x)

   [sin(60°) = 0.866, cos(60°) = 0.5, tan(60°) = 1.732]

3. Find $\cos^{-1}(\sin(60°))$ = ?

   [30°]

4. If cos(x) = 0.5   Find angle x

   [x = 60°]

5. x = 45°   Find sin(x) cos(x) and tan(x)

   [sin(45°) = 0.707, cos(45°) = 0.707, tan(45°) = 1]

6. x = 15°   Find sin(x), cos(x), and tan(x)

   [sin(15°) = 0.259, cos(15°) = 0.966, tan(15°) = 0.268]

7. Find $\sin^{-1}(\cos(30°))$ = ?

   [x = 60°]

8. If sin(x) = 0.315   Find angle x

   [x = 18.4°]

9. x = 90°   Find sin(x), cos(x), and tan(x)

   [sin(90°) = 1, cos(90°) = 0, tan(90°) = undefined]

10. x = 150°   Find sin(x), cos(x), and tan(x)

    [sin(150°) = 0.5, cos(150°) = -0.866, tan(150°) = -0.577]

11. Find $\sin(\cos^{-1}(0.5))$ = ?

    [0.866]

12. If tan(x) = 0.425   Find angle x

[x = 23.03°]

13. x = 117°   Find sin(x), cos(x), and tan(x)

[sin(117°) = 0.891, cos(117°) = -0.454, tan(117°)= -1.96]

14. x = 34.5°   Find sin(x), cos(x), and tan(x)

[sin(34.5°) = 0.566, cos(34.5°) = 0.824, tan(34.5°) = 0.687]

15. Find $\sin^{-1}(\tan(17°))$ = ?

[17.8°]

16. If sin(x) = -0.5   Find angle x

[x = 210°, 330° or -30°]

17. x = 100°   Find sin(x), cos(x), and tan(x)

[sin(100°) = 0.985, cos(100°) = -0.174, tan(100°) = -5.67]

18. x = 0°   Find sin(x), cos(x), and tan(x)

[sin(0°) = 0, cos(0°) = 1, tan(0°) = 0]

19. Find $\tan^{-1}(\cos(70°))$ = ?

[18.88°]

20. If tan(x) = -0.245 Find angle x

[x = 166.2°, 346.2°, or -13.8°]

T2 LESSON: SIN X   SINE OF X   X IS AN ANGLE (DEGREES $^\circ$)

We will extend the definition of **SIN** to include all angles from 0° to 180°. In Tier 3 we will extend the definition to include all angles both positive and negative.

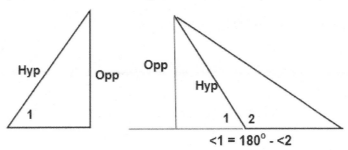

$$<1 = 180^\circ - <2$$

SIN(1) = Opp/Hyp   SIN(2) = Opp/Hyp = SIN(180° - <2)

If know two out of three, find the third, **Opp**, **Hyp**, (1)

Opp = SIN(1)xHyp   Opp = SIN(2)xHyp

Hyp = Opp/SIN(1)   Hyp = Opp/SIN(2)

(1) = SIN^{-1}(Opp/Hyp)   (2) = SIN^{-1}(Opp/Hyp)

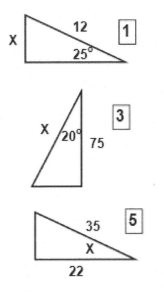

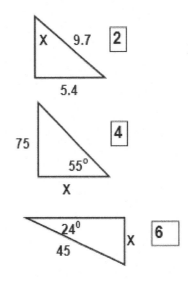

Answers: 1. 5.1   4. 52.5

2. 33.8° 5. 51.1°

3. 79.8   6. 18.3

Always set up the Equation first. Then solve.

Use the **Pythagorean Theorem** if necessary.

NOTE: Why is **Area** = .5ab**SIN**(<ab) correct?

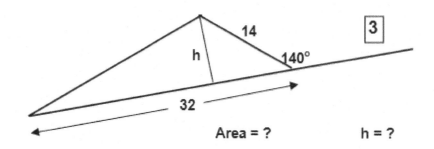

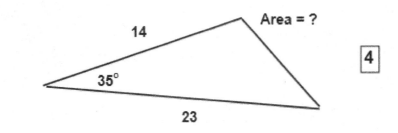

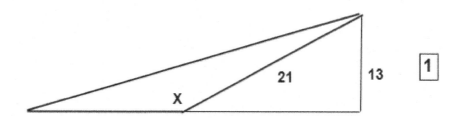

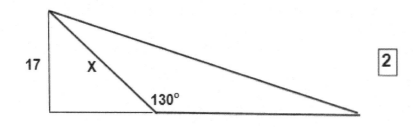

Answers: 1. 141.8°   3. A =144, h = 9
              2. 22.2   4. 92.3

SIN X   SINE OF X

X is an **angle** (degrees ^{o})

Find **x** in each of the following exercises.

1.
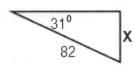

31^0

82

X

$$\boxed{x = ?}$$

2.
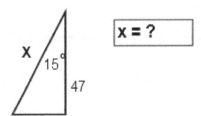

X

15°

47

$$\boxed{x = ?}$$

3.

X   11.2

6.3

$$\boxed{x = ?^0}$$

4.
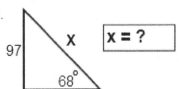

97

X

68°

$$\boxed{x = ?}$$

5.
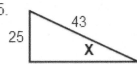

43

25

X

$$\boxed{x = ?^0}$$

6.
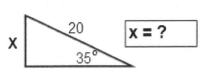

20

X

35°

$$\boxed{x = ?}$$

7.
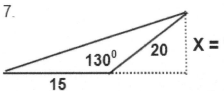

130^0 20

15

X = ?

Area of Triangle = ?

8.
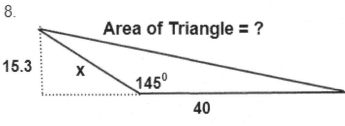

Area of Triangle = ?

15.3

X

145^0

40

x = ?

SIN X   SINE OF X

X is an **angle** (**degrees** $^{\circ}$)

Find **x** in each of the following exercises

1.
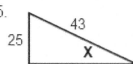
31^{0}
82
X

X = 42.2

2.
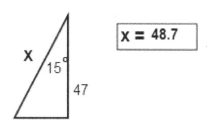
X
15°
47

X = 48.7

3.
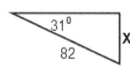
X   11.2
6.3

X = 34.2^{0}

4.

X
97
68°

X = 104.6

5.
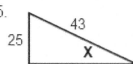
43
25
X

X = 35.5^{0}

6.
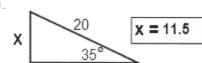
20
X
35°

X = 11.5

7.
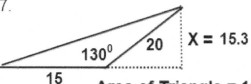
130^{0} 20
15

X = 15.3

Area of Triangle = 115 = 0.5x15x20xSIN(130^{0}) = 0.5x15x15.3

sin(50^{0})=x/20   x = sin(50^{0})x20 = 15.3

8.
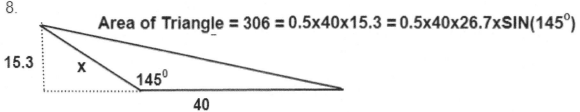
Area of Triangle = 306 = 0.5x40x15.3 = 0.5x40x26.7xSIN(145^{0})

15.3
X
145^{0}
40

X = 26.7

SIN X   SINE OF X

Find X in the following exercises.

1.

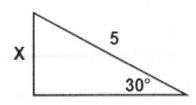

2.

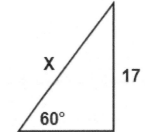

3.

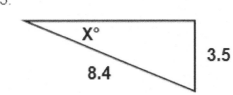

4.

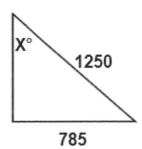

5.

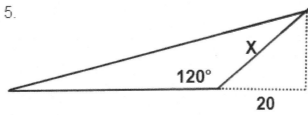

SIN X   SINE OF X

Find X in the following exercises.

1.

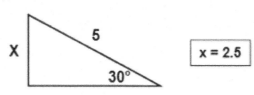

x = 2.5

2.

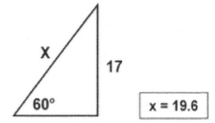

x = 19.6

3.

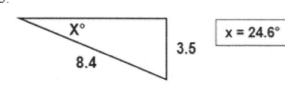

x = 24.6°

4.

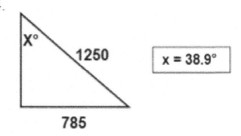

x = 38.9°

5.

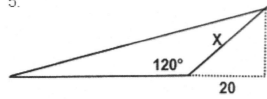

x = 40

T3 LESSON: COS X COSINE OF X. X IS AN ANGLE (DEGREES ^{o})

We will extend the definition of **COS** to include all angles from 0° to 180°. In Tier 3 we will extend the definition to include all angles both positive and negative.

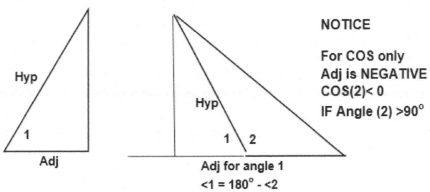

NOTICE

For COS only
Adj is NEGATIVE
COS(2)< 0
IF Angle (2) >90°

$COS(1) = Adj/Hyp$ $COS(2) = Adj/Hyp$ $COS(2) = -COS(180^{o} - <1)$

If you know two out of three, find the third, **Opp**, **Hyp**, **(1)**

$Adj = COS(1) \times Hyp$ $Adj = COS(2) \times Hyp$

$Hyp = Adj/COS(1)$ $Hyp = Adj/COS(2)$

$(1) = COS^{-1}(Adj/Hyp)$ $(2) = COS^{-1}(Adj/Hyp)$ $Adj < 0$

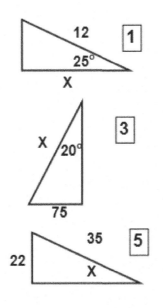

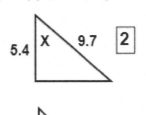

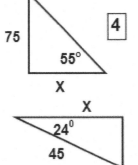

Answers:
   1. 10.9   2. 56.2^{o} 3. 219
   4. 52.5   5. 38.9^{o} 6. 41.1

T3 COS Problems

Always set up the Equation first. Then solve.

Use the **Pythagorean Theorem** if necessary.

NOTE: $COS(1) < 0$ IF $180° > (1) > 90°$

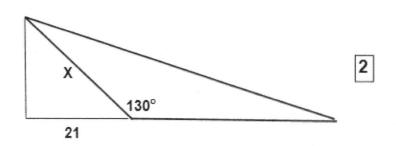

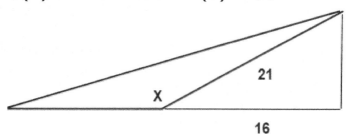

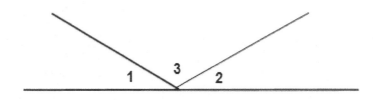

$<1 = <2$ and $<1 + <3 + <2 = 180°$

$<1 = 35°$ What does **COS**$(<2 + <3) = $?   3

$<3 = 120°$ What are **COS**(1) and **COS**$(2 + 3)$?   4

$<2 = 30°$ What are **SIN**(3) and **COS**(3) ?   5

Answers: 1. 137°   2. 32.7   3. -0.819
                  4. 0.866, -0.866   5. 0.866, -0.5

COS X COSINE OF X. X IS AN ANGLE (DEGREES $^{\circ}$)

Find **x** in the following exercises.

1.

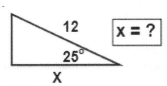

12

25°

X

x = ?

2.

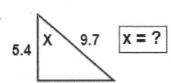

X   9.7

5.4

x = ?

3.

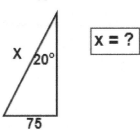

X   20°

75

x = ?

4.

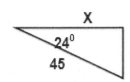

75

55°

X

x = ?

5.

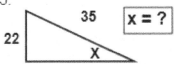

35

22

X

x = ?

6.

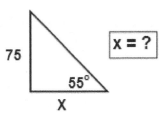

X

24^{0}

45

x = ?

7.

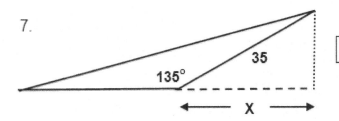

135°

35

⟵   X   ⟶

x = ?

COS X COSINE OF X. X IS AN ANGLE (DEGREES ^{o})

Find **x** in the following exercises.

1.

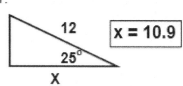

12   x = 10.9

25°

X

2.

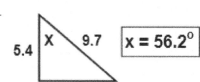

5.4   X   9.7   x = 56.2^{o}

3.

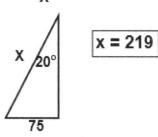

x = 219

X   20°

75

4.

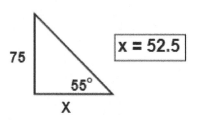

x = 52.5

75

55°

X

5.

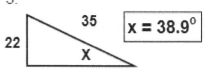

35   x = 38.9^{o}

22

X

6.

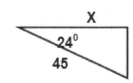

X

24°   x = 41.1

45

7.

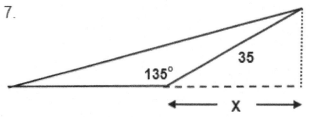

x = 24.7

35

135°

X

COS X COSINE OF X. X IS AN ANGLE (DEGREES $^{\circ}$)

Find X in the following exercises.

1.

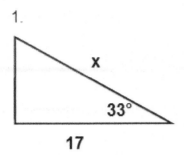

X

33°

17

2.

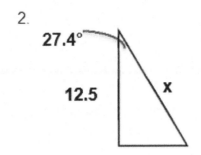

27.4°

12.5

X

3.

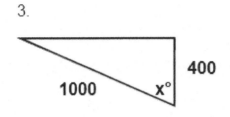

400

1000

x°

4.

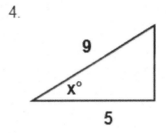

9

x°

5

5.

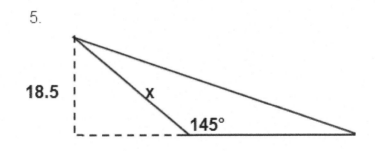

18.5

X

145°

COS X COSINE OF X. X IS AN ANGLE (DEGREES $^\circ$)

Find X in the following exercises.

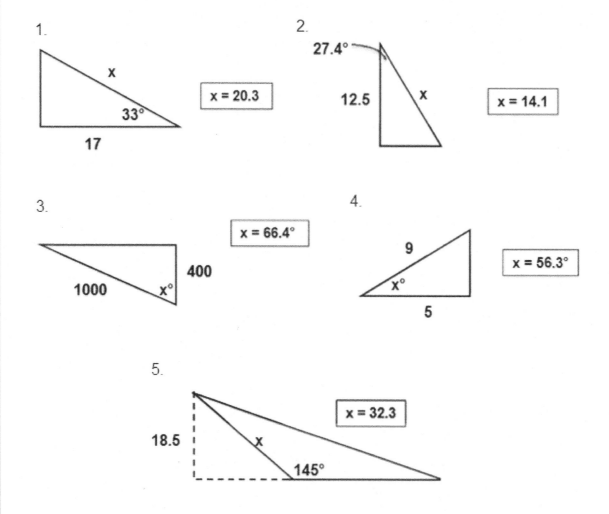

1.

x

33°

17

x = 20.3

2.

27.4°

12.5   x

x = 14.1

3.

400

1000   x°

x = 66.4°

4.

9

x°

5

x = 56.3°

5.

18.5

x

145°

x = 32.3

T4 LESSON: TAN X TANGENT OF X. X IS AN ANGLE (DEGREES ^{O})

TAN X can take on all values positive and negative

TAN X is **Not** defined at X = -90° or 90° (**Error**)

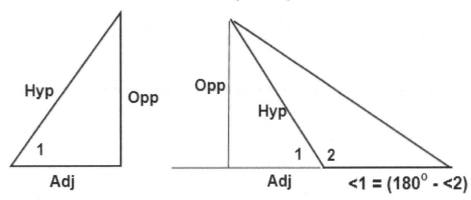

$$TAN(1) = Opp/Adj \qquad TAN(2) = Opp/Adj = -TAN(180^o - <2)$$

If know two out of three, find the third,   Opp,   Adj,   (1)

Opp = TAN(1)xAdj	Opp = TAN(2)xAdj	Adj < 0
Adj = Opp/TAN(1)	Adj = Opp/TAN(2)	Adj < 0

$$(1) = TAN^{-1}(Opp/Adj) \quad (2) = TAN^{-1}(Opp/Adj)$$

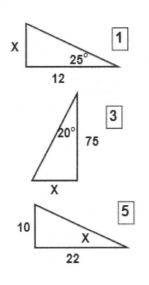

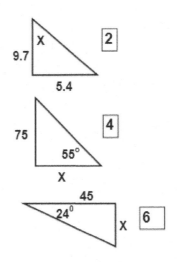

Answers: 1. 5.6   2. 29.1^o 3. 27.3
              4. 52.5   5. 24.4^o 6. 20.0

TAN X TANGENT OF X. X IS AN ANGLE (DEGREES $^{\circ}$)

Find X in each of the following exercises.

1.

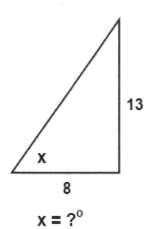

13

X

8

x = ?$^{\circ}$

2.

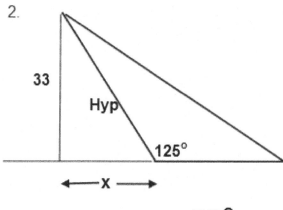

33

Hyp

125°

←—X—→

x = ?

3.

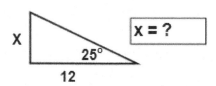

X

25°

12

x = ?

4.

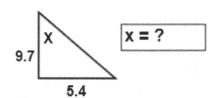

X

9.7

5.4

x = ?

5.

X = ?

20°

75

X

6.

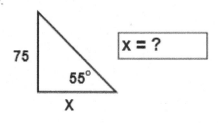

75

55°

X

x = ?

7.

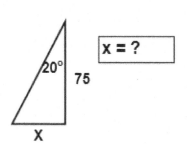

10

X

22

x = ?

8.

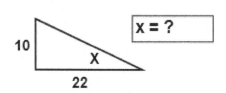

45

24^{0}

X

x = ?

TAN X TANGENT OF X. X IS AN ANGLE (DEGREES $^{\circ}$)

Find X in each of the following exercises.

1.
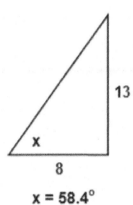
13

8

x = 58.4°

2.
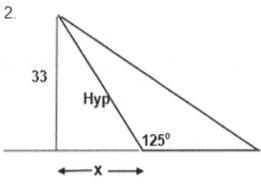
33

Hyp

125°

←X→

x = 23.1

3.
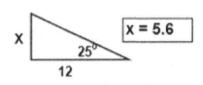
X

25°

12

x = 5.6

4.

9.7

X

5.4

x = 29.1°

5.
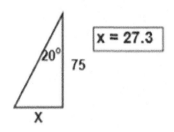
20°

75

X

x = 27.3

6.
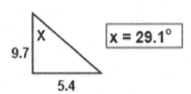
75

55°

X

x = 52.5

7.
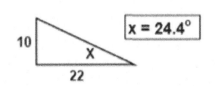
10

X

22

x = 24.4°

8.
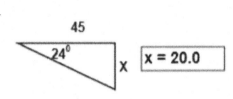
45

24°

X

x = 20.0

TAN X TANGENT OF X. X IS AN ANGLE (DEGREES $^{\circ}$)

Find X in each of the following exercises.

1.

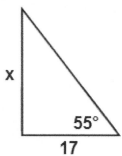

x

55°

17

2.

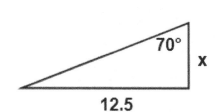

70°

x

12.5

3.

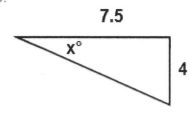

7.5

x°

4

4.

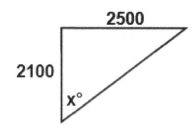

2500

2100

x°

5.

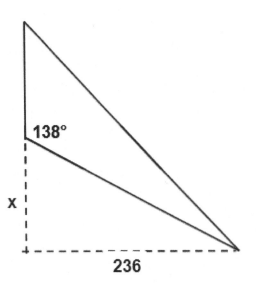

138°

x

236

TAN X TANGENT OF X. X IS AN ANGLE (DEGREES $^{\circ}$)

Find X in each of the following exercises.

1.

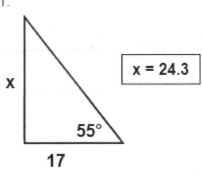

x = 24.3

x

55°

17

2.

x = 4.55

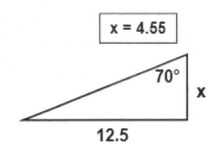

70°

x

12.5

3.

x = 28.1°

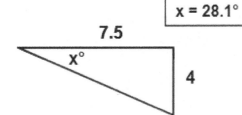

7.5

x°

4

4.

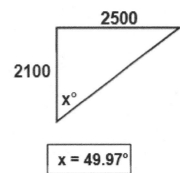

2500

2100

x°

x = 49.97°

5.

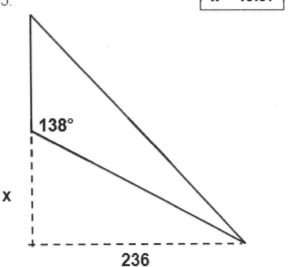

138°

x = 262.1

x

236

T5 LESSON: WARNING ABOUT SIN^{-1}

We are interested in **angles**, <A, from 0° to 180°

$SIN(<A) = SIN(180^o - <A)$ (see Table below)

So, if we have a **triangle** with an **angle** $<A > 90^o$, with $SIN(<A)$, then its SIN^{-1} will be wrong.

See below for example:

Suppose we know $SIN(<A) = .95105$, yet $SIN^{-1}(.95105) = 72^o$

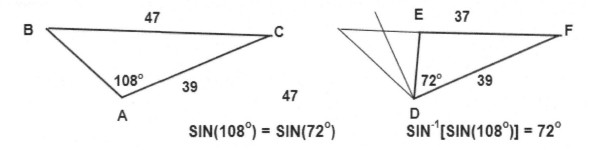

$SIN(108^o) = SIN(72^o)$ $SIN^{-1}[SIN(108^o)] = 72^o$

Angle <A	SIN(<A)	SIN⁻¹	Angle <A	COS(<A)	COS⁻¹
0	0.000	0	0	1.000	0
10	0.174	10	10	0.985	10
20	0.342	20	20	0.940	20
30	0.500	30	30	0.866	30
40	0.643	40	40	0.766	40
50	0.766	50	50	0.643	50
60	0.866	60	60	0.500	60
70	0.940	70	70	0.342	70
80	0.985	80	80	0.174	80
90	1.000	90	90	0.000	90
100	0.985	80	100	-0.174	100
110	0.940	70	110	-0.342	110
120	0.866	60	120	-0.500	120
130	0.766	50	130	-0.643	130
140	0.643	40	140	-0.766	140
150	0.500	30	150	-0.866	150
160	0.342	20	160	-0.940	160
170	0.174	10	170	-0.985	170
180	0.000	0	180	-1.000	180

WARNING ABOUT SIN^{-1}

When dealing with **angles** whose measure is between 90° and 180°, what happens with the **SIN** and **COS** which can lead to confusion?

If **X** is an angle between 90° and 180° how do **SIN** and **COS** behave?

Answer: Give examples:

? For **COS**

? For **SIN**

Suppose we know **SIN(<A) = 0.95105**, which triangle could this apply to?

Answer: ?

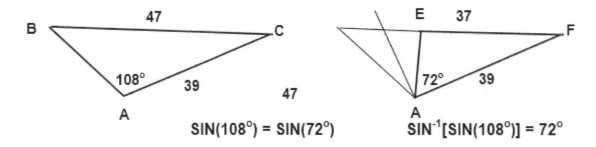

SIN(108°) = SIN(72°)   SIN^{-1}[SIN(108°)] = 72°

Suppose we know **COS(<A) = 0.3090**, which triangle could this apply to?

Answer: ?

WHY?

Answer: ?

WARNING ABOUT SIN^{-1}

When dealing with angles whose measure is between 90° and 180°, what happens with the **SIN** and **COS** which can lead to confusion?

If **X** is an angle between 90° and 180° how do **SIN** and **COS** behave?

　　Answer:　　　　　　　　　Give examples:

$COS(X°) = -COS(180° - X°)$　$COS(137°) = -COS(43°)$

　　　$SIN(X°) = SIN(180° - X°)$　　　$SIN(137°) = SIN(43°)$

Suppose we know **SIN**(<A) = 0.95105, which triangle could this apply to?

　　Answer:　Both

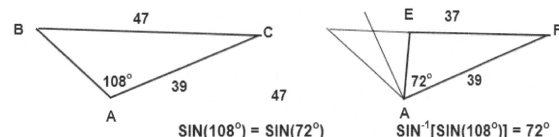

SIN(108°) = SIN(72°)　　　SIN^{-1}[SIN(108°)] = 72°

Suppose we know **COS**(<A) = 0.3090, which triangle could this apply to?

　　　　Answer:　Only Triangle **AEF**

WHY?

　　　　Answer:　**COS** (108°) = -0.3090

WARNING ABOUT SIN^{-1}

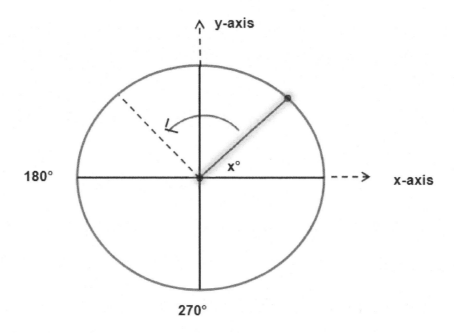

In the diagram above, the highlighted line rotates around in a circle in the xy-plane, starting at 0° and ending at 360°. Fill in the + or -

	0-90°	90-180°	180-270°	270-360°
sin(x)				
cos(x)				
tan(x)				

WARNING ABOUT SIN⁻¹

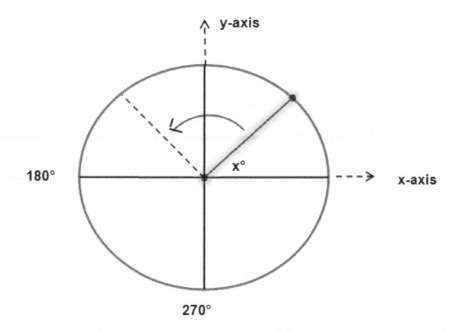

In the diagram above, the highlighted line rotates around in a circle in the xy-plane, starting at 0° and ending at 360°. Fill in the + or -

	0-90°	90-180°	180-270°	270-360°
sin(x)	positive	positive	negative	negative
cos(x)	positive	negative	negative	positive
tan(x)	positive	negative	positive	negative

T6 LESSON: LAW OF SINES

Problem: Suppose you have a triangle with two angles measuring $40°$ and $100°$ and the side opposite the $40°$ angle is 16 inches.

What is the length, **X**, of the side opposite the $100°$ angle? Look at the figure below.

Clearly **X** is larger than 16 in. Hmmm...maybe it is just proportional to the angles: How about:

$$X = (100°/40°)×16 = (5/2)×16 = 40 ?$$

Construct such a triangle and measure it, and you find it measures about 241/2 inches. SO; no, this doesn't work.

Hmmm...what could we do? How about trying some type of correction factor? How about taking the **SIN** of both angles?

$$SIN(100°)/SIN(40°)×16 = 24.5 \qquad \textbf{Eureka!} \quad ??$$

Could this always work? Answer: **YES**.

[SIN(<A)/SIN(<B)]xb = a, **ALWAYS**, for any angles.

Where **a** is opposite <A and **b** opposite <B

This is called the **Law of Sines**. We prove it in **Tier 3**.

We use it for practical problems. It makes "solving" **triangles** "child's play," especially with a **TI 30XA**.

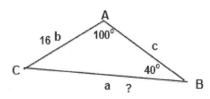

Law of Sines
$a/SIN(<A) = b/SIN(<B) = c/SIN(<C)$
$[SIN<A/SIN<B] \times b = a$

If you know two angles and an opposite side, you can find them all.

If you know two sides and an opposite angle you can find them all. Sometimes two possibilities.

Makes solving problems "child's play."

Still, if you know two sides and the included angle, we can't solve for the third side. Need one more tool.

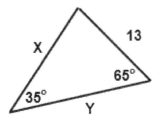

X/SIN(65°) = 13/SIN(35°), X = 20.5

Y/SIN(80°) = 13/SIN(35°), Y = 22.3

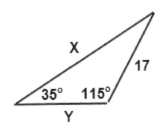

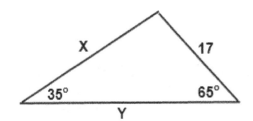

X/SIN(115°) = 17/SIN35°)	X/SIN(65°) = 17/SIN35°)
X = 26.9	X = 26.9
Y = 14.8	Y = 29.2

Observe: 115° + 65° = 180° Thus: SIN(115°) = SIN(65°)

Find X

Find X

Got to recognize limitations

Need One More Tool

LAW OF SINES

Find the Unknowns and answer questions.

1.

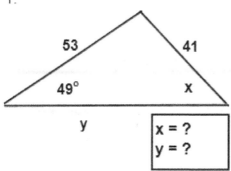

53   41

49°   x

y

x = ?
y = ?

2.

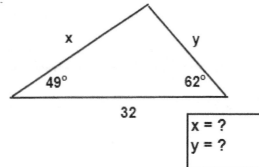

x   y

49°   62°

32

x = ?
y = ?

3.

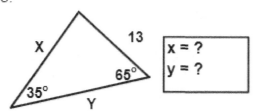

X   13

35°   65°

Y

x = ?
y = ?

4.

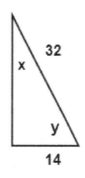

32

x

y

14

x = ?
y = ?

5.

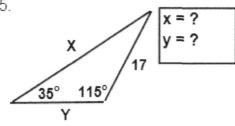

x = ?
y = ?

X

17

35°   115°

Y

6.

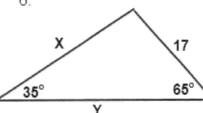

X   17

35°   65°

Y

x = ?
y = ?

7.

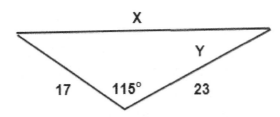

X

Y

17   115°   23

x = ?
y = ?

LAW OF SINES

Find the unknowns and answer questions.

1.

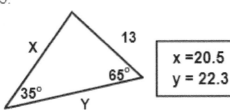

53   41

49°   x

y

x = 77.3°
y = 43.8

2.

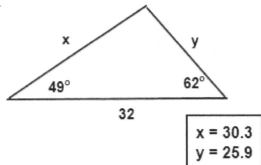

x   y

49°   62°

32

x = 30.3
y = 25.9

3.

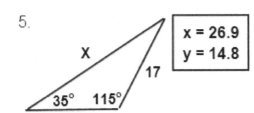

X   13

65°

35°   Y

x =20.5
y = 22.3

4.

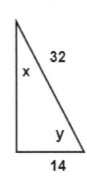

32

x

y

14

x = 25.9°
y = 64.1°

5.

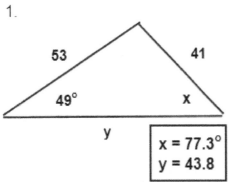

X

17

35°   115°

Y

x = 26.9
y = 14.8

6.

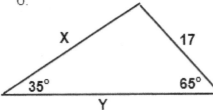

X   17

35°   65°

Y

x = 26.9
y = 29.2

7.

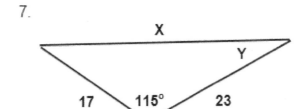

X

Y

17   115°   23

Can not find x and y with
tools given so far.
See T7 for solution.

LAW OF SINES

Find X and Y in the following exercises.

1.

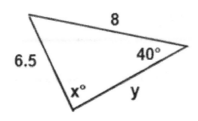

2.

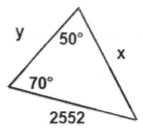

3.

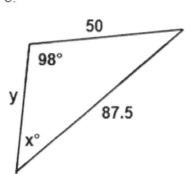

4.

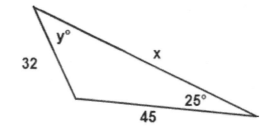

5.

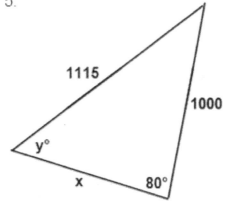

LAW OF SINES

Find X and Y in the following exercises.

1.

8

40°

6.5

x°   y

x = 52.3°
y = 10.1

2.

y   50°

x

70°

2552

x = 3130.5
y = 2885.1

3.

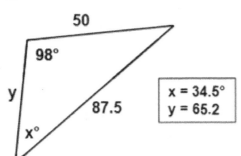

50

98°

y

87.5

x°

x = 34.5°
y = 65.2

4.

y°   x

32

25°

45

x = 66.5
y = 36.5°

5.

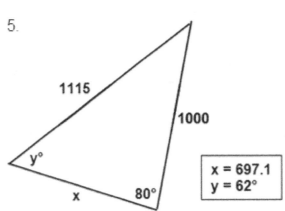

1115

1000

y°

x   80°

x = 697.1
y = 62°

T7 LESSON: LAW OF COSINES - GENERALIZED PYTHAGOREAN THEOREM

Suppose we know two sides and the included **angle** of a **triangle**. How can we calculate third side's length?

Easy if the **angle** is 90°. $c^2 = a^2 + b^2$

We need a **"correction factor"** for non-right **angles**,

$<a,b$ $c^2 = a^2 + b^2 - 2ab\textbf{COS}(<a,b)$, works for all **triangles**.

Also, let us find the **angles** when we only know the three sides of a **triangle**.

$<a,b = \textbf{COS}^{-1}[(a^2 + b^2 - c^2)/(2ab)]$, where $<a,b$ is included angle.

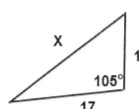

$X^2 = 17^2 + 13^2 - 2\text{x}13\text{x}17\text{x}\textbf{COS}105^\circ$

13   Thus, X = 23.9   **NOTE: COS**105° = -.2589, so CF is +

Thus, X = 16.9

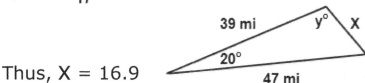

$X^2 = 39^2 + 47^2 - 2\text{x}39\text{x}47\text{x}\textbf{COS}20^\circ$

mi

Now we can also calculate y° Use **Law of Sines**
$y^\circ = 72^\circ$ or $(180^\circ - 72^\circ) = 108^\circ$

Clearly from the diagram 108° is correct.

Find the Area of the 3, 4, 6 triangle using A = .5abSIN(<a,b)

First, we must calculate $<a,b$ where a = 3, b = 4

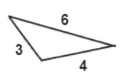

$<3,4 = \textbf{COS}^{-1}[(3^2 + 4^2 - 6^2)/(2\text{x}3\text{x}4)] = 117.3^\circ$

Area = $.5\text{x}\textbf{SIN}(117.3^\circ)\text{x}3\text{x}4 = 5.33$ U^2

LAW OF COSINES - GENERALIZED PYTHAGOREAN THEOREM

Find the Unknowns

Start with the problem we could not solve in T6

1.

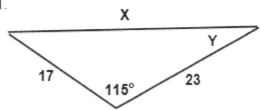

x = ?
y = ?

2.

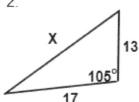

x = ?

3.

x = ?
y = ?

4. Find the Area of this triangle

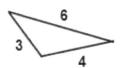

LAW OF COSINES - GENERALIZED PYTHAGOREAN THEOREM

Find the Unknowns

Start with the problem we could not solve in T6

1.
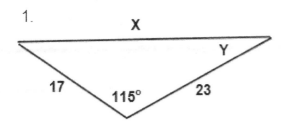

$$x = 33.9$$
$$y = 27°$$

$$x^2 = 17^2 + 23^2 - 2 \times 17 \times 23 \times COS(115°)$$
$$y = SIN^{-1}[\{SIN(115°)/33.9\} \times 17]$$

2.
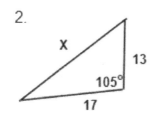

$$X^2 = 17^2 + 13^2 - 2 \times 13 \times 17 \times COS105°$$

Thus, X = 23.9   NOTE: $COS105° = -0.2589$, so, **CF** is **+**

3.
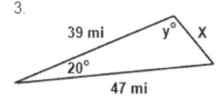

$$X^2 = 39^2 + 47^2 - 2 \times 39 \times 47 \times COS20°$$

Thus, X = 16.9 mi

Now we can also calculate $y°$

Use **Law of Sines**

Clearly from the diagram $108°$ is correct. $y° = 72°$ or
$$(180° - 72°) = 108°$$

Find the Area of the 3, 4, 6 triangle using A = .5abSIN(<a,b)

First, we must calculate <a,b where a = 3, b = 4

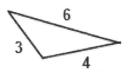

$$<3,4 = COS^{-1}[(3^2 + 4^2 - 6^2)/(2 \times 3 \times 4)] = 117.3°$$

Area = $.5 \times SIN(117.3°) \times 3 \times 4 = 5.33$ U^2

LAW OF COSINES

Find X and Y in the following exercises.

1.

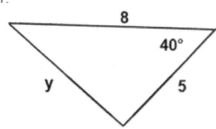

2.

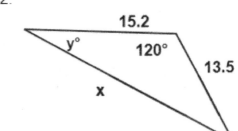

3.

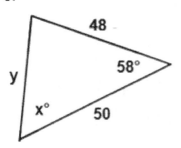

4.

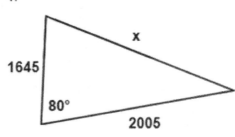

5.

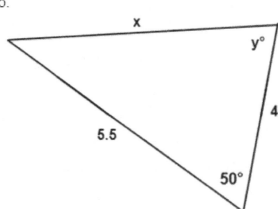

AREAS OF IRREGULAR TRIANGLES

6.

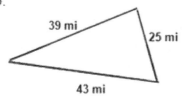

39 mi
25 mi
43 mi

7.

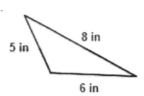

8 in
5 in
6 in

8.

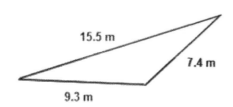

15.5 m
7.4 m
9.3 m

9.

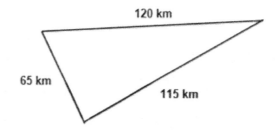

120 km
65 km
115 km

LAW OF COSINES

Find X and Y in the following exercises.

1.

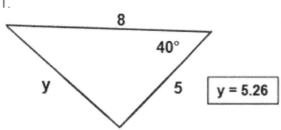

8

40°

y   5

y = 5.26

2.

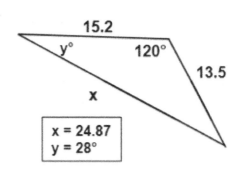

15.2

y°   120°

13.5

x

x = 24.87
y = 28°

3.

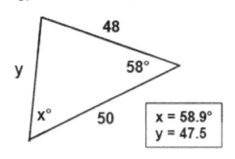

48

58°

y

x°   50

x = 58.9°
y = 47.5

4.

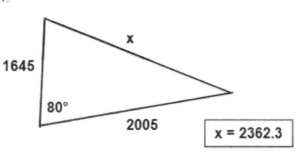

x

1645

80°

2005

x = 2362.3

5.

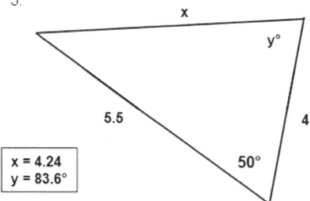

x

y°

5.5

4

50°

x = 4.24
y = 83.6°

LAW OF COSINES

6.

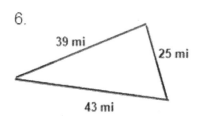

39 mi

25 mi

43 mi

A = 481.8 mi²

7.

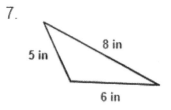

8 in

5 in

6 in

A = 14.98 in²

8.

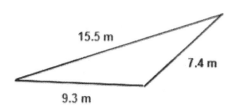

15.5 m

7.4 m

9.3 m

A = 23.9 m²

9.

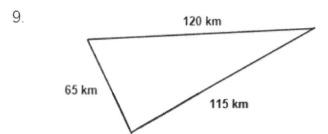

120 km

65 km

115 km

A = 3,659 km²

T8 LESSON: TRIGONOMETRY BEYOND PRACTICAL MATH (OPTIONAL)

Trigonometry is a huge extremely important subject with profound applications in science and engineering.

The **Trig Functions** are called the **Circle Functions** and are defined for **ALL** angles, both positive and negative.

Trig Functions are very important in **calculus**.

Trig Functions are probably best understood in the context of the Complex Number System.

Trig Functions are the basis of modern spectrometry via what is called the **Fourier Transform**.

The **Trig Functions** are periodic and that is what makes them so important in any type of **cyclical behavior** such as vibration analysis, and music.

So next, you will need to understand the **Trig functions** via graphs in analytical geometry (Tier 3).

Then one needs to learn about them in the context of the Complex Number System. That is when many of the famous **Trig Identities** will become very natural and understandable. What I consider the most important equation in all of mathematics makes this clear (Tier 4).

Then one needs to learn about their behavior utilizing the **calculus**. It is truly amazing (Tier 5).

Ultimately, they are profound in Functional Analysis and modern physics such as **Quantum Theory** (Tier 9).

TRIGONOMETRY BEYOND PRACTICAL MATH (OPTIONAL)

Trigonometry is a huge extremely important subject with profound applications in science and engineering and advanced mathematics.

If you are planning to study math beyond Practical Math, then you should be aware of some of the future applications of **Trigonometry**.

List as many things you have heard about where **Trig** will be useful and applicable.

If you study other resources such as Wikipedia you will probably come up with other applications in addition to those I have pointed out.

Please accept my best wishes for your future success.

I hope mathematics will be rewarding to you in your future endeavors, and enjoyable too.

Thank you for studying this **Foundations Course**.

Dr. Del.

TRIGONOMETRY BEYOND PRACTICAL MATH (OPTIONAL)

Trigonometry is a huge extremely important subject with profound applications in science and engineering.

The **Trig Functions** are called the **Circle Functions** and are defined for **ALL** angles, both positive and negative.

Trig functions are very important in **calculus**.

Trig Functions are probably best understood in the context of the Complex Number System.

Trig Functions are the basis of modern spectrometry via what is called the **Fourier Transform**.

The **Trig Functions** are periodic and that is what makes them so important in any type of **cyclical behavior** such as vibration analysis, and music.

So next, you will need to understand the **Trig Functions** via graphs in analytical geometry (Tier 3).

Then one needs to learn about them in the context of the Complex Number System. That is when many of the famous **Trig Identities** will become very natural and understandable. What I consider the most important equation in all of mathematics makes this clear (Tier 4).

Then one needs to learn about their behavior utilizing the **calculus**. It is truly amazing (Tier 5).

Ultimately, they are profound in **Functional Analysis** and modern physics such as **Quantum Theory** (Tier 9).

Made in United States
Orlando, FL
10 June 2023

34014448R00128